WILLIAM SHAKESPEARE was ...on-
Avon in April, 1564, and his birth ...ted
on April 23. The facts of his life, ...g doc-
uments, are sparse. He was one of eight children born to
John Shakespeare, a merchant of some standing in his community. William probably went to the King's New School in
Stratford, but he had no university education. In November
1582, at the age of eighteen, he married Anne Hathaway,
eight years his senior, who was pregnant with their first
child, Susanna. She was born on May 26, 1583. Twins, a boy,
Hamnet (who would die at age eleven), and a girl, Judith,
were born in 1585. By 1592 Shakespeare had gone to London, working as an actor and already known as a playwright. A rival dramatist, Robert Greene, referred to him as
"an upstart crow, beautified with our feathers." Shakespeare became a principal shareholder and playwright of
the successful acting troupe the Lord Chamberlain's men
(later, under James I, called the King's men). In 1599 the
Lord Chamberlain's men built and occupied the Globe Theatre in Southwark near the Thames River. Here many of
Shakespeare's plays were performed by the most famous
actors of his time, including Richard Burbage, Will Kempe,
and Robert Armin. In addition to his 37 plays, Shakespeare
had a hand in others, including *Sir Thomas More* and *The
Two Noble Kinsmen*, and he wrote poems, including *Venus
and Adonis* and *The Rape of Lucrece*. His 154 sonnets were
published, probably without his authorization, in 1609. In
1611 or 1612 he gave up his lodgings in London and devoted
more and more of his time to retirement in Stratford,
though he continued writing such plays as *The Tempest* and
Henry VIII until about 1613. He died on April 23, 1616, and
was buried in Holy Trinity Church, Stratford. No collected
edition of his plays was published during his lifetime,
but in 1623 two members of his acting company, John
Heminges and Henry Condell, published the great collec-
tion now called the First Folio.

Bantam Shakespeare
28 Volumes
Edited by David Bevington
With forewords by Joseph Papp on the plays

The Poems: Venus and Adonis, The Rape of Lucrece, The
Phoenix and Turtle, A Lover's Complaint,
the Sonnets

Antony and Cleopatra	*The Merchant of Venice*
As You Like It	*A Midsummer Night's Dream*
The Comedy of Errors	*Much Ado about Nothing*
Hamlet	*Othello*
Henry IV, Part One	*Richard II*
Henry IV, Part Two	*Richard III*
Henry V	*Romeo and Juliet*
Julius Caesar	*The Taming of the Shrew*
King Lear	*The Tempest*
Macbeth	*Twelfth Night*

Together in one volume:

Henry VI, Parts One, Two, and Three
King John and Henry VIII
Measure for Measure, All's Well that Ends Well, and
Troilus and Cressida
Three Early Comedies: Love's Labor's Lost, The Two
Gentlemen of Verona, The Merry
Wives of Windsor
The Late Romances: Pericles, Cymbeline, The Winter's
Tale, The Tempest

Two collections:

Four Comedies: The Taming of the Shrew, A Midsummer
Night's Dream, The Merchant of Venice,
Twelfth Night
Four Tragedies: Hamlet, Othello, King Lear, Macbeth

William Shakespeare

HENRY IV, PART ONE

Edited by
David Bevington

David Scott Kastan,
James Hammersmith,
and Robert Kean Turner,
Associate Editors

With a Foreword by
Joseph Papp

BANTAM BOOKS
TORONTO / NEW YORK / LONDON / SYDNEY / AUCKLAND

HENRY IV, PART ONE

*A Bantam Book / published by arrangement
with Scott, Foresman and Company*

PUBLISHING HISTORY

*Scott, Foresman edition published January 1980
Bantam edition, with newly edited text and substantially revised,
edited, and amplified notes, introductions, and other
materials / February 1988
Valuable advice on staging matters has been
provided by Richard Hosley.
Collations checked by Eric Rasmussen.
Additional editorial assistance by Claire McEachern.*

ISBN 0-553-21293-1

Published simultaneously in the United States and Canada

*Bantam Books are published by Bantam Books, a division of Random House, Inc.
Its trademark, consisting of the words "Bantam Books" and the portrayal of a
rooster, is Registered in U.S. Patent and Trademark Office and in other countries.
Marca Registrada. Bantam Books, 1540 Broadway, New York, New York 10036.*

PRINTED IN THE UNITED STATES OF AMERICA

OPM   10

Contents

Foreword

It's hard to imagine, but Shakespeare wrote all of his plays with a quill pen, a goose feather whose hard end had to be sharpened frequently. How many times did he scrape the dull end to a point with his knife, dip it into the inkwell, and bring up, dripping wet, those wonderful words and ideas that are known all over the world?

In the age of word processors, typewriters, and ballpoint pens, we have almost forgotten the meaning of the word "blot." Yet when I went to school, in the 1930s, my classmates and I knew all too well what an inkblot from the metal-tipped pens we used would do to a nice clean page of a test paper, and we groaned whenever a splotch fell across the sheet. Most of us finished the school day with ink-stained fingers; those who were less careful also went home with ink-stained shirts, which were almost impossible to get clean.

When I think about how long it took me to write the simplest composition with a metal-tipped pen and ink, I can only marvel at how many plays Shakespeare scratched out with his goose-feather quill pen, year after year. Imagine him walking down one of the narrow cobblestoned streets of London, or perhaps drinking a pint of beer in his local alehouse. Suddenly his mind catches fire with an idea, or a sentence, or a previously elusive phrase. He is burning with impatience to write it down—but because he doesn't have a ballpoint pen or even a pencil in his pocket, he has to keep the idea in his head until he can get to his quill and parchment.

He rushes back to his lodgings on Silver Street, ignoring the vendors hawking brooms, the coaches clattering by, the piteous wails of beggars and prisoners. Bounding up the stairs, he snatches his quill and starts to write furiously, not even bothering to light a candle against the dusk. "To be, or not to be," he scrawls, "that is the—." But the quill point has gone dull, the letters have fattened out illegibly, and in the middle of writing one of the most famous passages in the history of dramatic literature, Shakespeare has to stop to sharpen his pen.

Taking a deep breath, he lights a candle now that it's dark, sits down, and begins again. By the time the candle has burned out and the noisy apprentices of his French Huguenot landlord have quieted down, Shakespeare has finished Act 3 of *Hamlet* with scarcely a blot.

Early the next morning, he hurries through the fog of a London summer morning to the rooms of his colleague Richard Burbage, the actor for whom the role of Hamlet is being written. He finds Burbage asleep and snoring loudly, sprawled across his straw mattress. Not only had the actor performed in *Henry V* the previous afternoon, but he had then gone out carousing all night with some friends who had come to the performance.

Shakespeare shakes his friend awake, until, bleary-eyed, Burbage sits up in his bed. "Dammit, Will," he grumbles, "can't you let an honest man sleep?" But the playwright, his eyes shining and the words tumbling out of his mouth, says, "Shut up and listen—tell me what you think of *this*!"

He begins to read to the still half-asleep Burbage, pacing around the room as he speaks. ". . . Whether 'tis nobler in the mind to suffer the slings and arrows of outrageous fortune—"

Burbage interrupts, suddenly wide awake, "That's excellent, very good, 'the slings and arrows of outrageous fortune,' yes, I think it will work quite well. . . ." He takes the parchment from Shakespeare and murmurs the lines to himself, slowly at first but with growing excitement.

The sun is just coming up, and the words of one of Shakespeare's most famous soliloquies are being uttered for the first time by the first actor ever to bring Hamlet to life. It must have been an exhilarating moment.

Shakespeare wrote most of his plays to be performed live by the actor Richard Burbage and the rest of the Lord Chamberlain's men (later the King's men). Today, however, our first encounter with the plays is usually in the form of the printed word. And there is no question that reading Shakespeare for the first time isn't easy. His plays aren't comic books or magazines or the dime-store detective novels I read when I was young. A lot of his sentences are complex. Many of his words are no longer used in our everyday speech. His profound thoughts are often condensed into poetry, which is not as straightforward as prose.

Yet when you hear the words spoken aloud, a lot of the language may strike you as unexpectedly modern. For Shakespeare's plays, like any dramatic work, weren't really meant to be read; they were meant to be spoken, seen, and performed. It's amazing how lines that are so troublesome in print can flow so naturally and easily when spoken.

I think it was precisely this music that first fascinated me. When I was growing up, Shakespeare was a stranger to me. I had no particular interest in him, for I was from a different cultural tradition. It never occurred to me that his plays might be more than just something to "get through" in school, like science or math or the physical education requirement we had to fulfill. My passions then were movies, radio, and vaudeville—certainly not Elizabethan drama.

I was, however, fascinated by words and language. Because I grew up in a home where Yiddish was spoken, and English was only a second language, I was acutely sensitive to the musical sounds of different languages and had an ear for lilt and cadence and rhythm in the spoken word. And so I loved reciting poems and speeches even as a very young child. In first grade I learned lots of short nature verses— "Who has seen the wind?," one of them began. My first foray into drama was playing the role of Scrooge in Charles Dickens's *A Christmas Carol* when I was eight years old. I liked summoning all the scorn and coldness I possessed and putting them into the words, "Bah, humbug!"

From there I moved on to longer and more famous poems and other works by writers of the 1930s. Then, in junior high school, I made my first acquaintance with Shakespeare through his play *Julius Caesar*. Our teacher, Miss McKay, assigned the class a passage to memorize from the opening scene of the play, the one that begins "Wherefore rejoice? What conquest brings he home?" The passage seemed so wonderfully theatrical and alive to me, and the experience of memorizing and reciting it was so much fun, that I went on to memorize another speech from the play on my own.

I chose Mark Antony's address to the crowd in Act 3,

scene 2, which struck me then as incredibly high drama.
Even today, when I speak the words, I feel the same thrill I
did that first time. There is the strong and athletic Antony
descending from the raised pulpit where he has been speaking, right into the midst of a crowded Roman square. Holding the torn and bloody cloak of the murdered Julius
Caesar in his hand, he begins to speak to the people of
Rome:

> If you have tears, prepare to shed them now.
> You all do know this mantle. I remember
> The first time ever Caesar put it on;
> 'Twas on a summer's evening in his tent,
> That day he overcame the Nervii.
> Look, in this place ran Cassius' dagger through.
> See what a rent the envious Casca made.
> Through this the well-belovèd Brutus stabbed,
> And as he plucked his cursèd steel away,
> Mark how the blood of Caesar followed it,
> As rushing out of doors to be resolved
> If Brutus so unkindly knocked or no;
> For Brutus, as you know, was Caesar's angel.
> Judge, O you gods, how dearly Caesar loved him!
> This was the most unkindest cut of all . . .

I'm not sure now that I even knew Shakespeare had written a lot of other plays, or that he was considered "time-
less," "universal," or "classic"—but I knew a good speech
when I heard one, and I found the splendid rhythms of
Antony's rhetoric as exciting as anything I'd ever come
across.

Fifty years later, I still feel that way. Hearing good actors
speak Shakespeare gracefully and naturally is a wonderful
experience, unlike any other I know. There's a satisfying
fullness to the spoken word that the printed page just can't
convey. This is why seeing the plays of Shakespeare performed live in a theater is the best way to appreciate them.
If you can't do that, listening to sound recordings or watch-
ing film versions of the plays is the next best thing.

But if you do start with the printed word, use the play as a
script. Be an actor yourself and say the lines out loud. Don't
worry too much at first about words you don't immediately
understand. Look them up in the footnotes or a dictionary,

but don't spend too much time on this. It is more profitable (and fun) to get the sense of a passage and sing it out. Speak naturally, almost as if you were talking to a friend, but be sure to enunciate the words properly. You'll be surprised at how much you understand simply by speaking the speech "trippingly on the tongue," as Hamlet advises the Players.

You might start, as I once did, with a speech from *Julius Caesar*, in which the tribune (city official) Marullus scolds the commoners for transferring their loyalties so quickly from the defeated and murdered general Pompey to the newly victorious Julius Caesar:

> Wherefore rejoice? What conquest brings he home?
> What tributaries follow him to Rome
> To grace in captive bonds his chariot wheels?
> You blocks, you stones, you worse than senseless
>   things!
> O you hard hearts, you cruel men of Rome,
> Knew you not Pompey? Many a time and oft
> Have you climbed up to walls and battlements,
> To towers and windows, yea, to chimney tops,
> Your infants in your arms, and there have sat
> The livelong day, with patient expectation,
> To see great Pompey pass the streets of Rome.

With the exception of one or two words like "wherefore" (which means "why," not "where"), "tributaries" (which means "captives"), and "patient expectation" (which means patient waiting), the meaning and emotions of this speech can be easily understood.

From here you can go on to dialogues or other more challenging scenes. Although you may stumble over unaccustomed phrases or unfamiliar words at first, and even fall flat when you're crossing some particularly rocky passages, pick yourself up and stay with it. Remember that it takes time to feel at home with anything new. Soon you'll come to recognize Shakespeare's unique sense of humor and way of saying things as easily as you recognize a friend's laughter.

And then it will just be a matter of choosing which one of Shakespeare's plays you want to tackle next. As a true fan of his, you'll find that you're constantly learning from his plays. It's a journey of discovery that you can continue for the rest of your life. For no matter how many times you read or see a particular play, there will always be something new there that you won't have noticed before.

Why do so many thousands of people get hooked on Shakespeare and develop a habit that lasts a lifetime? What can he really say to us today, in a world filled with inventions and problems he never could have imagined? And how do you get past his special language and difficult sentence structure to understand him?

The best way to answer these questions is to go see a live production. You might not know much about Shakespeare, or much about the theater, but when you watch actors performing one of his plays on the stage, it will soon become clear to you why people get so excited about a playwright who lived hundreds of years ago.

For the story—what's happening in the play—is the most accessible part of Shakespeare. In *A Midsummer Night's Dream*, for example, you can immediately understand the situation: a girl is chasing a guy who's chasing a girl who's chasing another guy. No wonder *A Midsummer Night's Dream* is one of the most popular of Shakespeare's plays: it's about one of the world's most popular pastimes—falling in love.

But the course of true love never did run smooth, as the young suitor Lysander says. Often in Shakespeare's comedies the girl whom the guy loves doesn't love him back, or she loves him but he loves someone else. In *The Two Gentlemen of Verona*, Julia loves Proteus, Proteus loves Sylvia, and Sylvia loves Valentine, who is Proteus's best friend. In the end, of course, true love prevails, but not without lots of complications along the way.

For in all of his plays—comedies, histories, and tragedies—Shakespeare is showing you human nature. His characters act and react in the most extraordinary ways—and sometimes in the most incomprehensible ways. People are always trying to find motivations for what a character does. They ask, "Why does Iago want to destroy Othello?"

The answer, to me, is very simple—because that's the way Iago is. That's just his nature. Shakespeare doesn't explain his characters; he sets them in motion—and away they go. He doesn't worry about whether they're likable or not. He's interested in interesting people, and his most fascinating characters are those who are unpredictable. If you lean back in your chair early on in one of his plays, thinking you've figured out what Iago or Shylock (in *The Merchant of Venice*) is up to, don't be too sure—because that great judge of human nature, Shakespeare, will surprise you every time.

He is just as wily in the way he structures a play. In *Macbeth*, a comic scene is suddenly introduced just after the bloodiest and most treacherous slaughter imaginable, of a guest and king by his host and subject, when in comes a drunk porter who has to go to the bathroom. Shakespeare is tickling your emotions by bringing a stand-up comic on-stage right on the heels of a savage murder.

It has taken me thirty years to understand even some of these things, and so I'm not suggesting that Shakespeare is immediately understandable. I've gotten to know him not through theory but through practice, the practice of the *living* Shakespeare—the playwright of the theater.

Of course the plays are a great achievement of dramatic literature, and they should be studied and analyzed in schools and universities. But you must always remember, when reading all the words *about* the playwright and his plays, that *Shakespeare's* words came first and that in the end there is nothing greater than a single actor on the stage speaking the lines of Shakespeare.

Everything important that I know about Shakespeare comes from the practical business of producing and directing his plays in the theater. The task of classifying, criticizing, and editing Shakespeare's printed works I happily leave to others. For me, his plays really do live on the stage, not on the page. That is what he wrote them for and that is how they are best appreciated.

Although Shakespeare lived and wrote hundreds of years ago, his name rolls off my tongue as if he were my brother. As a producer and director, I feel that there is a professional relationship between us that spans the centuries. As a human being, I feel that Shakespeare has enriched my understanding of life immeasurably. I hope you'll let him do the same for you.

✧

Henry IV, Part One is a continuation of *Richard II*, and it was interesting for me to direct both in one season in 1987. If the main focus in *Richard* was the relationship between Bolingbroke and the King, *1 Henry IV* revolves around three central characters—Falstaff, Prince Hal, and Hotspur. This trio determines the tone of the entire play, and it's important to make sure that the three harmonize and complement each other as they should. The casting of the trio can be problematic, because it's not just a question of getting any three actors, but three actors who "fit" together. It's a triangle full of possibilities for both directors and actors.

Of the three, Falstaff rules—or misrules—the play, for one of the same reasons that Richard II rules his play, his command of language. This unregenerate rogue blusters his way through the play, getting himself out of every predicament with his shrewdness and wit. Unlike the Falstaff of *The Merry Wives of Windsor*, who is a victim of others' shrewdness, here Falstaff indisputably reigns in the Eastcheap setting of *1 Henry IV;* no matter what tricks are played on him, he manages to rise above them. Gradually, as the *Henry IV* saga unfolds in *Part Two* he'll become less and less capable of doing so, but for the duration of this play, he is irrepressible.

JOSEPH PAPP

JOSEPH PAPP GRATEFULLY ACKNOWLEDGES THE HELP OF ELIZABETH KIRKLAND IN PREPARING THIS FOREWORD.

HENRY IV,
PART ONE

Introduction

The opening of *1 Henry IV* is taut and grave in tone. England is "shaken" and "wan with care." The troubles of *Richard II*, to which this play (c. 1596–1597) is a close sequel, have not been left behind. However much King Henry would prefer to unite his countrymen against a common foreign enemy in a crusade to the holy lands, he is prevented from doing so by continuing civil war. The impassioned rhetoric of his opening speech proclaiming a new era of peace can only end in anticlimax, for the actual purpose of this meeting in council is to receive and assess reports of military action against the throne.

Henry's current troubles are in the far reaches of his kingdom: Scots in the north, Welsh in the west. Fighting for Henry on these two fronts are the nobles of the Percy family who helped him to power: Harry Percy (Hotspur), his father (Henry Percy) the Earl of Northumberland, his uncle the Earl of Worcester, and his brother-in-law Edmund Mortimer the Earl of March. Apparently they have fought bravely. Yet we soon sense that all is not well between the new king and those who rebelled with him against Richard II. A quarrel breaks out because Hotspur refuses to deliver to Henry some prisoners as required by feudal obedience. The matter of the ransom money is only a technicality; what is really at issue? In part, it is Henry's insistence on being obeyed on principle. Admiring Hotspur inordinately, the King feels he must discipline affectionately this fine young warrior as a father would discipline his son. Even more deeply, however, the issue of the prisoners galls Henry because of the proviso that he ransom Mortimer, captured by the Welsh. Henry has not forgotten that Mortimer is his chief rival for the English crown, being descended from the Duke of Clarence (elder brother to Henry's father, Gaunt), and having been proclaimed by Richard heir to the throne. Mortimer is the last person Henry would wish ransomed. Moreover, the King suspects Mortimer of having fought with something less than total zeal against the Welsh Glendower. News of Mortimer's marriage to Glendower's daughter confirms the King's worst fears.

Henry knows Northumberland and Worcester to be expert in treasonous plotting, since they conspired with him to overthrow Richard. Now, Henry believes, these Percys are extending their alliance by a series of calculated marriages in order to seize power once again. This time their claimant is Mortimer.

Shakespeare's sympathies are many-sided. The Percy clan is in fact organizing against Henry, but not without cause. As they see it, the man they helped to the throne has done little for them since. His manner of disciplining them sounds too much like hostility and ingratitude. Other counselors attend the King constantly, while Worcester is banished from court. In such an atmosphere of distrust, suspicion breeds still more suspicion. The situation has polarized, surely more than either party originally intended.

Hotspur is the most attractive of the rebels, to us as well as to King Henry. He is outspoken, courageous, witty, domineering in conversation. Above all, he is a disciple of manliness, loyalty, chivalry, bravery in battle—the attributes of an upstanding and somewhat old-fashioned sense of honor. Yet a fatal defect dwells among these attractive qualities. Hotspur is impatient, proud, unwilling to tolerate a rival— be it Glendower or Prince Hal (Henry, Prince of Wales). In his first speech, purporting to explain his refusal to deliver the prisoners, he brilliantly satirizes an effete courtier who had come to him from King Henry in the midst of a battle. The satire betrays many harsh qualities in Hotspur: the self-indulgent wrath that returns fully to him even in recollection of the encounter, the pride in his own stoical indifference to suffering, and especially the obsessive nature (revealed in the repetitive pattern of the rhetoric) of his contempt for courtiers generally. Surely his scorn for stay-at-home politicians is directed in part at King Henry himself. To Hotspur all courtiers are effeminate, perfume-wearing, affected in mannerism and speech, scarcely masculine. This preoccupation of Hotspur's makes him extraordinarily prone to one-sided judgments. Like most excessive devotees of chivalry, he divides mankind into two categories: those who are gentlemen, like himself, and those who are beneath contempt. The "vile politician" Bolingbroke and his son the "sword-and-buckler Prince of Wales" (1.3.240, 229) fall into the latter category.

Prone as he is to such an overly simple view of political behavior, Hotspur can see no good in the King's cause and no evil in his own. He is a poor listener because of his obsession and yet an easy prey for his uncle and father, who require his leadership for their cause. They need only implant the suggestion that King Henry is acting from a political motive in his refusal to ransom Mortimer, and Hotspur is ready to leap incautiously to the defense of their cause. The great irony is that Hotspur fails to see political motives in the machinations of his own relatives. While he fights for bright honor, they maneuver cautiously for position and prove uncertain allies when the hour of battle approaches. Most crucially, they betray Hotspur in the prebattle negotiations, at which he is not present. As Worcester explains to Vernon during their return to rebel headquarters (5.2.3–25), they cannot let Hotspur know of the King's offer to settle matters by a general pardon. Although, as they realize, the King could pardon Hotspur's youth, there can be no turning back for themselves. Thus the honor for which Hotspur fights is at bottom a lie, and the mutual esteem that might have grown between him and a much-reformed Prince of Wales is thwarted by the polarization of attitudes in the two camps. Hotspur's brand of honor is the victim of its own excess, and lends some credence to Falstaff's wry conclusion that honor "is a mere scutcheon" (5.1.139–140).

The contrasting of Falstaff and Hotspur on the theme of honor suggests that they are dramatic foils for each other, representing extremes between which Prince Hal must choose. Shakespeare uses this foil device structurally and consciously; for example, he has considerably reduced the age of the Hotspur he found in Raphael Holinshed's *Chronicles* (1578) in order to accentuate the similarity between Hotspur and Hal. Conversely, to emphasize the contrast between Falstaff and Hotspur, Shakespeare envisages Falstaff as old (nearly sixty, by his own admission), fat, humorous, and without honor. Falstaff's vices are Hotspur's virtues, and the reverse. Whereas Hotspur offers to Hal a model of chivalric striving and attention to duty, Falstaff is a highwayman and liar. On the other hand, Hotspur is a fanatic, unbending and self-absorbed even in the company of his sprightly wife, Kate, irritated by music and poetry; Falstaff is the epitome of merriment and joie de vivre. We excuse much in him because he lusts after life with such an appetite, and ingratiates himself to others by inviting them to laugh at his expense.

Despite the nearly irresistible attractiveness of Falstaff as a jolly companion and butt of humorous joking, his conversations with Prince Hal are, from their first moments together, involved with the issue of Hal's ultimate rejection of Falstaff. The witty raillery of their first scene (1.2) seems designed to provide diverting entertainment for the Prince and for us, and yet beneath the gay surface we perceive that Hal and Falstaff are talking about the hanging of thieves and the question of whether or not Hal should give in to sinful temptation. Can the relationship of Hal and Falstaff continue unchanged into the reign of Henry V? Will there be gallows standing and justice for highwaymen? Will "Monsieur Remorse," as Poins calls Falstaff, ever sincerely repent? Will the Prince, for that matter? To allay our fears, Hal soliloquizes at scene's end, vowing his determination to use these scapegrace companions as mere foils for his triumphal reformation at the appropriate time. But this explanation raises an opposite danger in our sympathies: Is he callously using his companions merely to create a self-serving myth of Prince Hal, the Politician with the Common Touch? Is Francis the drawer no more to Hal than a butt for his raillery? Since the rejection of Falstaff is, by Hal's own words, already determined, can we credit him with a serious friendship? Where do Shakespeare's sympathies lie, with the need for political order or with the hedonistic spirit of youth? Perhaps he recognizes the validity of both, and accordingly shows us a prince who is genuinely fond of Falstaff's exuberant company, but who also knows that he is a king's son and must sooner or later accept the consequences of that unsought role. Falstaff's gift to him is youthful irresponsibility, which must be cherished (by all of us) even though it cannot last.

In the Gad's Hill robbery, Falstaff reveals that his "cowardice" differs from the natural craven fear of Bardolph and Peto. He fights no longer than he sees "reason," that is, not against such unfair odds as two athletic young men in the dark (or later, at Shrewsbury, against the burly Scots giant, the Douglas). A man could get killed that way. Falstaff's cowardice, then, is philosophic, seen by himself in a humorous perspective. The same is true of his lying about the robbery. However much Hal exults in exposing Falstaff as a fraud, we cannot dismiss the possibility that Falstaff may see through the Prince's scheme and then feed Hal the expectedly outlandish lie (two men in buckram become eleven men) as a means of begging for affection. Falstaff's only way of pleading his cause is to tickle the Prince's fancy, in his role as a kind of court fool. What Falstaff most wants is to be loved and retained for what he is; and that, poignantly enough, is the one thing the mature Henry V cannot grant.

Throughout *1 Henry IV*, Shakespeare seems interested in the relationships between fathers and sons. These relationships help structure the comparisons and contrasts among foil characters. Falstaff is a foil not only for Hotspur, but also for Henry IV; that is, despite all his insistence on youthful irresponsibility, Falstaff acts as a kind of parental figure to Hal. In the tavern scene (2.4), Falstaff and Hal take turns playing king and crown prince, and in both roles Falstaff wittily argues his case as companion and guide to the heir to the throne. Is it better to be old and merry, fat and loved, or to be hated like Pharaoh's lean kine? Falstaff argues against the gravity of council meetings with the same amused fervor he later directs at the grinning honor of a dead hero. Hal, in his turn as king, questions the propriety of a "devil" haunting the crown prince "in the likeness of an old fat man," a "reverend Vice," a "gray Iniquity," a "father ruffian" (2.4.442–449). For all the good humor in this exchange, both men are asking whether Falstaff or King Henry serves Hal as the better model. Hal anticipates some of the very arguments his father will use against him next day at court, and indeed the insistent presence of that sober adult world makes itself felt even in the tavern. To Falstaff's moving litany, urging that Hal "banish not him thy Harry's company—banish plump Jack, and banish all the world," the Prince can only reply, "I do, I will" (ll. 472–476).

Hotspur too is regarded as a son by more than one father. King Henry only half-jokingly wishes it could be proved that some night-tripping fairy had exchanged his Harry in the cradle for Harry Percy (1.1.85–89). Paradoxically, the King admires Hotspur all the more for standing up to him, just as another imperious father figure, Owen Glendower, bestows grudging but real admiration on Hotspur for his outspokenness (3.1.1–185). Hotspur's rebellious ways are cherished because they seem to promise manliness and fame; Hal's rebellious ways are feared and despised because they seem to reject the values of duty and leadership on which King Henry bases his self-respect. In these terms, the play must resolve Hal's coming of age, his acceptance of his role as true son of the King and his proving his worth to the King. Hal must find his adult self, a self that differs greatly from that of King Henry, but must do so in a way that preserves the integrity of their relationship and the real debt he owes his father.

These conflicts reach their climax and resolution at the field of Shrewsbury in Act 5. Hal's worth must be proven at Hotspur's expense. The rivalry between the two has been intense throughout the play, as seen for example in Hal's brilliant mimicking of Hotspur's devotion to bloodshed (2.4.101–108). Aware that his tarnished reputation puts him at a disadvantage, Hal speaks nobly of his rival and impresses even the adversary camp with his regal bearing (5.1.83–100, 5.2.51–68). He rescues his father in the battle, thereby proving to King Henry that his son does not wish to supplant him as he had feared. After the battle, Hal frees his Scottish adversary the Douglas in a display of princely magnificence, doing so with a more generous motive than Hotspur had displayed in his earlier release of the Douglas as his prisoner (1.3.259–262). Meantime, Hal has put considerable distance between himself and Falstaff, though sensitive still to the warmth of old memories. When he sees Hotspur and Falstaff on the ground together, both seemingly dead, Hal views as in a tableau the contrasting models between which he has shaped his own identity. Yet Falstaff is not dead. He rises to mutilate Hotspur's body and to claim the honor due Hal for Hotspur's death. For all Falstaff's witty commentary at the expense of honor, his own opposite course is unsuited to a time of war or to Hal's new public role. Falstaff's abuse of military conscription, his carrying a bottle of sack in place of a pistol, show him at his wittiest still, but in a world that may not tolerate such pranks. The merry games are out of place, childish. With characteristic generosity and imprudence, Hal gives the credit for Hotspur's death to Falstaff who claims it so cravenly. Even so, the magic of their association has vanished. The time of manhood is upon Hal.

Henry IV, Part One
in Performance

1 Henry IV enjoyed an instant success in the late 1590s, owing especially to the appeal of Falstaff, and has remained popular onstage ever since. Though certainly it was acted in the public theater, the first recorded performance is one in 1600 for the Flemish Ambassador, Louis Verreyken, at Essex House, and it appeared several more times at court before the Interregnum of the mid-seventeenth century when the theaters were closed. Its early popularity is confirmed by Leonard Digges's assertion in his prefatory verse for the 1640 edition of Shakespeare's *Poems:* "let but Falstaff come, / Hal, Poins, the rest, you scarce shall have a room, / All is so pestered."

A shortened version or "droll" called *The Bouncing Knight, or The Robbers Robbed* was shown surreptitiously during the Interregnum, and the play itself was soon revived on the Restoration stage. The diarist Samuel Pepys saw at least parts of *1 Henry IV* on four occasions during the 1660s. Thomas Betterton as Falstaff took London by storm in the 1699–1700 season, after earlier successes with the part of Hotspur, which he played, according to Colley Cibber, with "fierce and flashing fire." James Quin played Hotspur at the theater in Lincoln's Inn Fields, London, in 1718 and then, like Betterton, shifted to the role of Falstaff for his greatest triumphs in the play in 1721 and after. John Henderson, Thomas Ryder, and John Fawcett, Jr., were among the many popular Falstaffs of the eighteenth century. At the Haymarket Theatre in 1786, Lydia Webb chose to play the fat knight for her benefit performance, but the experiment did not meet with critical approval: "every joke was delivered with a sort of sententious dignity," the *Morning Chronicle* reported, "that destroyed its natural impression."

In the early nineteenth century, the roles of Falstaff and Hotspur continued to dominate productions of the play and attract the leading actors of the day, often in very broad interpretation. George Frederick Cooke, in 1802 at the Theatre Royal, Covent Garden, acted Falstaff "like an old lurching sharper," according to the editor of the *London Sun*. John Philip Kemble's heavyset brother, Stephen, was the most acclaimed Falstaff of the era, acting the role between 1802 and 1820, usually in tandem with his famous sibling as Hotspur, though in 1819 and 1820 he played opposite Edmund Kean. William Charles Macready played Hotspur to appreciative audiences between 1815 and 1847. When Queen Victoria requested a revival two years after Macready's last performance in the role, he politely declined, claiming that his age made him unfit for the part. For sheer spectacle, the most eye-catching production of the early nineteenth century was Charles Kemble's monumental *1 Henry IV* in 1824 at Covent Garden. With scrupulous and perhaps overly realistic attention to the accuracy of the historical reconstruction (Henry IV, for example, was dressed according to an effigy of that monarch in Canterbury Cathedral), Kemble's elaborate production gained considerable attention. Kemble's Falstaff disappointed or surprised some spectators who did not think his usual graceful and courtly style well suited to an old, fat rogue who must "lard the lean earth" as he walks along. Samuel Phelps was perhaps an equally unlikely Falstaff in his production at the Sadler's Wells Theatre in 1846 (at least one critic thought he could use "a little more stuffing"), though he managed to succeed in the role by emphasizing Falstaff's shrewdness and caustic wit.

Charles Kemble and Phelps were among the very few exceptions to the prevailing tendency in the eighteenth and nineteenth centuries to portray Falstaff through slapstick and even coarse stage business, making of him a buffoon and comic scapegoat. Productions often exploited his ungainly corpulence. The American actor James Henry Hackett, appearing often as Falstaff in a long career from 1832 to 1870, interpreted the old, fat sinner as an epitome of vanity and vice. Once, when Hackett appeared onstage in Edinburgh with his famous artificially inflated belly, he was attacked by a pin-wielding fellow actor wishing to deflate the egocentric star. During the Gad's Hill robbery (2.2), the Falstaff of this era often incongruously pranced about in wild excitement as he defied his victims. Sitting down to divide the spoils with his comrades, and being set upon by Hal and Poins, Falstaff inevitably found he was unable to get up, and so he had to crawl to safety at considerable cost to his dignity. In the long tavern scene (2.4) he was apt to throw the dregs of his sack in Francis's face and play the business of being caught out in a lie with the resourcefulness of a practiced liar. At Shrewsbury Field, before the battle (5.1), Falstaff was sometimes directed to sit on a drum next to Henry IV and then tumble off when the King suddenly got up. When Falstaff fell down in battle to avoid the might of the Douglas (5.4), he made no attempt to convince the spectators that he was really dead in order that he might surprise them by coming again to life; instead, he dodged his head about, winked, started to get up only to duck down nervously at the sound of approaching military activity, and generally played the situation for broad laughs. Falstaff's difficulty in getting the dead Hotspur on his back became so great at times that his comic crew, Bardolph, Peto, and the rest, had to help lug off the corpse. Not all these routines were included in any single performance, but cumulatively they do indicate the extent to which Falstaff was played as a comic butt, a coward, and a liar.

The demeaning nature of this comedy helps explain why Maurice Morgann, in his *Essay on the Dramatic Character of Sir John Falstaff* (1777), felt it necessary to defend Falstaff as neither a liar nor a coward, but rather a vital, fascinating, and even courageous man. Morgann's sentimental apology was part of a literary rejection of the stage for the world of books, where Falstaff's wit could be savored as that of a companion and witty table guest, one whose seemingly craven behavior is only part of a self-aware repertory of antics designed to humor the Prince. Other devotees of Shakespeare during the Romantic period joined Morgann in admiring Falstaff's joie de vivre while disapproving of Prince Henry's calculated prudence and political pragmatism. Falstaff onstage in the early nineteenth century, contrastingly, was a corrupter of Hal's innocence. Seldom have the theater and literary worlds been so far apart.

Beginning in the early twentieth century, the modern theater has moved away from both the sentimental and the moralistic responses to character expressed in nineteenth-century criticism and stagecraft, finding instead, with the assistance of a full playing text and continuous action made possible by the abandonment of Victorian scenic elaboration, a balance between Falstaff's wit and the threat he poses to civil order. Padded with extensive wickerwork, Herbert Beerbohm Tree played an immense, jovial Falstaff in his productions in 1896 at the Haymarket Theatre and in 1914 at His Majesty's Theatre. The text was essentially unaltered, in a major departure from Tree's usual freewheeling practice. Matheson Lang stammered in his playing of Hotspur in the 1914 production, using a mannerism that was to become characteristic of later Hotspurs. (Lady Percy's reference in *2 Henry IV* to Hotspur's "speaking thick," from which Lang took his cue, probably means only that he spoke quickly.) Frank Benson directed an energetic *1 Henry IV* at Stratford-upon-Avon both in 1905 and in 1909, the last brilliantly balanced in sympathy between Louis Calvert's Falstaff, Lewis Waller's Hotspur, and Hal (played by Fred G. Worlock, though Benson himself played the role in 1905). Barry Jackson's imaginative direction of the play in the first season of the Birmingham Repertory Theatre in 1913 explored the parallels between the historical action and the tavern world through the uninterrupted transitions of locale possible on his permanent set. Russell Thorndike and Charles Warburton directed the play at the Old Vic in 1920, with Thorndike as Falstaff, in a swift, economical production that, like Nugent Monck's production at the small Maddermarket Theatre in Norwich in 1922 and Ben Iden Payne's at Stratford-upon-Avon in 1935, demonstrated the play's refusal, when unabridged and unelaborated, to allow any one of its characters to dominate the action. Indeed the full text, staged with "speed and simplicity," as critic W. A. Darlington put it in behalf of the new credo, drew its energy precisely from the lines of tension established by the balance of its three main characters. Hal's father, the careworn and aging king, added his perspective to the complex debate on statecraft and maturity as *1 Henry IV* was increasingly examined from its various angles of vision.

After World War II, these subtle tensions lent themselves to a new pertinence and a new emphasis directed at a world grown weary, even suspicious, of politicians and military heroes. Productions increasingly showed Hal's father as cold and Machiavellian and Hotspur as the tragic embodiment of an archaic if rigorous code of honor. Such was the case, for example, in the 1964 production at Stratford-upon-Avon directed by Peter Hall, John Barton, and Clifford Williams, in which Hugh Griffith's vitality as Falstaff was set off against the emotionally sterile world of politics and war embodied in a cold-blooded and self-aware Prince of Wales (Ian Holm). The battle scenes were deliberately frightening, not stylized or balletic; the strain and violence were always distressingly evident. Orson Welles's 1965 film *Chimes at Midnight* (called *Falstaff* in the United States) centered on the hurt of the rejection of Falstaff; Welles's Falstaff was funny but also poignant, always aware of the blow that was sure to fall.

Many recent productions have sought a complex sense of the play as a whole by focusing less on Falstaff as the comic antagonist of scheming politicians and more on the intricacies of relationship between Hal and Falstaff, Hal and his father, Hal and Hotspur. The range of interpretation has been considerable, suggesting the versatility of Shakespeare's script. In John Burrell's Old Vic production of 1945 at London's New Theatre, Ralph Richardson's sensitive and funny portrayal of Falstaff was set off against the fire and atmospherics of Laurence Olivier's Hotspur. Richard Burton's interpretation of Hal at Stratford-upon-Avon in 1951 found little room for merriment in a young man determined from the start to break with Falstaff. Alan Howard, similarly, played Hal, under the direction of Terry Hands at Stratford-upon-Avon in 1975, as joyless in his role as future king, delighted neither by Falstaff nor the possibilities of future rule. Conversely, in Gerald Freedman's production of the play for the New York Shakespeare Festival in 1968, Sam Waterston was an awkwardly attractive Prince unsure of what was expected of him, at once fascinated and repelled by Stacy Keach's comically smug Falstaff. Gerard Murphy portrayed Hal, in the Royal Shakespeare Company's production, directed by Trevor Nunn at the Barbican Theatre in 1982, as an immature young man clinging to Falstaff in defiance of his austere father. Murphy's Hal sat in Falstaff's lap during their first scene together and even cleaned up the mess that Falstaff had made of his breakfast. The Prince's reconciliation with his father was never complete. At Shrewsbury, Hal engaged with Hotspur in an exhausting and unchivalrous duel. Hal's choice, between an oppressive and guilt-ridden father and a waggish, genial companion whose claims on Hal were nonetheless disturbing in their insinuations of a claim of power, was not an easy one.

Balanced between the extremes of an unsmiling, politic prince and an emotionally dependent son, the performance of Robert Hardy, directed by Douglas Seale at the Old Vic in 1955, caught the two sides of Hal's maturation in a different and perhaps more sympathetic way. This Hal though always aware of the call of royal duty, entered into the life of the tavern with spontaneous enjoyment and hilarity until the press of national affairs could no longer be ignored. His turning away from Falstaff (Paul Rogers) was reluctant and loving, yet firmly resolved. Michael Bogdanov's modern-dress *1 Henry IV*, at the Old Vic in 1987 after a national tour the previous year, focused on the conflict in the world with which Hal must come to terms, by evoking with theatrical brilliance a culture in awkward transition from a stable world of traditional values to one that provided more room for opportunism and conscious self-fashioning. Michael Pennington's self-effacing Prince revealed both the patience and the guile that would make his rule successful.

Any production of *1 Henry IV* must find theatrical expression for the juxtaposed realms of experience called for in the play's script and originally designed for performance on the Elizabethan stage. As the opening scenes shift back and forth from royal court to Prince Hal's life with Falstaff, from high seriousness to comedy, the stage must alternately present scenes of taut negotiation and witty repartee. Falstaff's world burlesques that of the court: he is a kind of adviser to a prince, to be sure, but in him everything is inverted. On the Elizabethan stage or on the modern stage, Falstaff's comic world is essentially the world of the tavern, conjured up in the spectators' imagination by tables and chairs, by tapsters and tavern keepers, by knocks at the door, by extemporaneous playacting, by racy and colloquial language. With or without scenery, the tavern world defines itself theatrically by its festive atmosphere and its topsy-turvy presentation of everything serious in the world of political struggle.

The contrasts between court and tavern, though requiring no shift of elaborate sets, exploit a number of opportunities for recurrent visual effects to intensify the juxtaposition of two worlds, as when, in the long tavern scene (2.4), Falstaff mockingly assumes the "throne" and is then "deposed" by Prince Hal. When Hal goes to court the next morning to see his father, the memory of his hilarious rehearsal the night before adds immeasurably to the dimensions of generational conflict. Such parallels may well have been reinforced on Shakespeare's stage by parallel gesture and blocking. When Falstaff goes to war, in Act 5, the two worlds of political responsibility and carefree pleasure are at last jarringly drawn together; Hal's various role models are all present at the conflict. Perhaps the most arresting stage image of the choice Hal must make is at the moment of Hotspur's death, when Hal beholds the prostrate bodies of Falstaff and Hotspur, both seemingly dead, the one symbolizing honor and the other a hedonistic preference for life by whatever means necessary. Yet Hotspur is really dead; Falstaff survives, breaking through the very illusion of stage convention to rise from death as actors do at the end of a play. Playacting and serious action mingle on the field of Shrewsbury, hinting at the complex ways in which theater imitates life.

The Playhouse

This early copy of a drawing by Johannes de Witt of the Swan Theatre in London (c. 1596), made by his friend Arend van Buchell, is the only surviving contemporary sketch of the interior of a public theater in the 1590s.

From other contemporary evidence, including the stage directions and dialogue of Elizabethan plays, we can surmise that the various public theaters where Shakespeare's plays were produced (the Theatre, the Curtain, the Globe) resembled the Swan in many important particulars, though there must have been some variations as well. The public playhouses were essentially round, or polygonal, and open to the sky, forming an acting arena approximately 70 feet in diameter; they did not have a large curtain with which to open and close a scene, such as we see today in opera and some traditional theater. A platform measuring approximately 43 feet across and 27 feet deep, referred to in the de Witt drawing as the *proscaenium*, projected into the yard, *planities sive arena*. The roof, *tectum*, above the stage and supported by two pillars, could contain machinery for ascents and descents, as were required in several of Shakespeare's late plays. Above this roof was a hut, shown in the drawing with a flag flying atop it and a trumpeter at its door announcing the performance of a play. The underside of the stage roof, called the heavens, was usually richly decorated with symbolic figures of the sun, the moon, and the constellations. The platform stage stood at a height of $5\frac{1}{2}$ feet or so above the yard, providing room under the stage for underworldly effects. A trapdoor, which is not visible in this drawing, gave access to the space below.

The structure at the back of the platform (labeled *mimorum aedes*), known as the tiring-house because it was the actors' attiring (dressing) space, featured at least two doors, as shown here. Some theaters seem to have also had a discovery space, or curtained recessed alcove, perhaps between the two doors—in which Falstaff could have hidden from the sheriff (*1 Henry IV*, 2.4) or Polonius could have eavesdropped on Hamlet and his mother (*Hamlet*, 3.4). This discovery space probably gave the actors a means of access to and from the tiring-house. Curtains may also have been hung in front of the stage doors on occasion. The de Witt drawing shows a gallery above the doors that extends across the back and evidently contains spectators. On occasions when action "above" demanded the use of this space, as when Juliet appears at her "window" (*Romeo and Juliet*, 2.2 and 3.5), the gallery seems to have been used by the actors, but large scenes there were impractical.

The three-tiered auditorium is perhaps best described by Thomas Platter, a visitor to London in 1599 who saw on that occasion Shakespeare's *Julius Caesar* performed at the Globe:

> The playhouses are so constructed that they play on a raised platform, so that everyone has a good view. There are different galleries and places [*orchestra, sedilia, porticus*], however, where the seating is better and more comfortable and therefore more expensive. For whoever cares to stand below only pays one English penny, but if he wishes to sit, he enters by another door [*ingressus*] and pays another penny, while if he desires to sit in the most comfortable seats, which are cushioned, where he not only sees everything well but can also be seen, then he pays yet another English penny at another door. And during the performance food and drink are carried round the audience, so that for what one cares to pay one may also have refreshment.

Scenery was not used, though the theater building itself was handsome enough to invoke a feeling of order and hierarchy that lent itself to the splendor and pageantry onstage. Portable properties, such as thrones, stools, tables, and beds, could be carried or thrust on as needed. In the scene pictured here by de Witt, a lady on a bench, attended perhaps by her waiting-gentlewoman, receives the address of a male figure. If Shakespeare had written *Twelfth Night* by 1596 for performance at the Swan, we could imagine Malvolio appearing like this as he bows before the Countess Olivia and her gentlewoman, Maria.

HENRY IV,
PART ONE

[Dramatis Personae

KING HENRY THE FOURTH
PRINCE HENRY, *Prince of Wales,*
PRINCE JOHN OF LANCASTER, } *sons of the King*
EARL OF WESTMORLAND
SIR WALTER BLUNT

EARL OF NORTHUMBERLAND, *Henry Percy,*
HARRY PERCY (HOTSPUR), *his son,*
EARL OF WORCESTER, *Northumberland's*
  younger brother,
LORD MORTIMER, *Edmund Mortimer,*
  also referred to as the Earl of March,
OWEN GLENDOWER,
EARL OF DOUGLAS, *Archibald Douglas,*
SIR RICHARD VERNON,
ARCHBISHOP OF YORK, *Richard Scroop,*
SIR MICHAEL, *a member of the*
  Archbishop's household,

} *rebels against the King*

LADY PERCY, *Hotspur's wife and Mortimer's sister*
LADY MORTIMER, *Mortimer's wife and Glendower's daughter*

SIR JOHN FALSTAFF
NED POINS
BARDOLPH
PETO
GADSHILL, *arranger of the highway robbery*
HOSTESS *of the tavern, Mistress Quickly*
FRANCIS, *a drawer, or tapster*
VINTNER, *or tavern keeper*

FIRST CARRIER
SECOND CARRIER
HOSTLER
CHAMBERLAIN
FIRST TRAVELER
SHERIFF
SERVANT *to Hotspur*
MESSENGER
SECOND MESSENGER
Soldiers, Travelers, Lords, Attendants

SCENE: *England and Wales*]

1.1   *Enter the King, Lord John of Lancaster, [the]*
         Earl of Westmorland, [Sir Walter Blunt,] with
         others.

KING
   So shaken as we are, so wan with care,
   Find we a time for frighted peace to pant,   2
   And breathe short-winded accents of new broils   3
   To be commenced in strands afar remote.   4
   No more the thirsty entrance of this soil   5
   Shall daub her lips with her own children's blood;   6
   No more shall trenching war channel her fields   7
   Nor bruise her flowerets with the armèd hoofs
   Of hostile paces. Those opposèd eyes,   9
   Which, like the meteors of a troubled heaven,
   All of one nature, of one substance bred,
   Did lately meet in the intestine shock   12
   And furious close of civil butchery,   13
   Shall now, in mutual well-beseeming ranks,
   March all one way and be no more opposed
   Against acquaintance, kindred, and allies.
   The edge of war, like an ill-sheathèd knife,
   No more shall cut his master. Therefore, friends,   18
   As far as to the sepulcher of Christ—
   Whose soldier now, under whose blessèd cross
   We are impressèd and engaged to fight—   21
   Forthwith a power of English shall we levy,   22
   Whose arms were molded in their mother's womb   23
   To chase these pagans in those holy fields
   Over whose acres walked those blessèd feet
   Which fourteen hundred years ago were nailed
   For our advantage on the bitter cross.
   But this our purpose now is twelve month old,

1.1. Location: London. The royal court.
2 Find we let us find.   **frighted** frightened   **3 breathe short-winded
accents** speak even though we are out of breath.   **accents** words.
broils battles   **4 strands afar remote** far-off shores, i.e., of the Holy
Land (to which, at the end of *Richard II*, Henry has pledged himself to a
crusade)   **5 thirsty entrance** i.e., parched mouth   **6 daub** coat, smear
7 trenching cutting   **9 paces** horses' tread   **12 intestine** internal
13 close hand-to-hand encounter.   **civil** (as in "civil war")   **18 his** its
21 impressèd conscripted   **22 power** army   **23 their mother's** i.e.,
England's

And bootless 'tis to tell you we will go.   29
Therefor we meet not now. Then let me hear
Of you, my gentle cousin Westmorland,   31
What yesternight our Council did decree
In forwarding this dear expedience.   33

WESTMORLAND
My liege, this haste was hot in question,   34
And many limits of the charge set down   35
But yesternight, when all athwart there came   36
A post from Wales loaden with heavy news,   37
Whose worst was that the noble Mortimer,
Leading the men of Herefordshire to fight
Against the irregular and wild Glendower,
Was by the rude hands of that Welshman taken,
A thousand of his people butcherèd—
Upon whose dead corpse there was such misuse,   43
Such beastly shameless transformation,   44
By those Welshwomen done as may not be
Without much shame retold or spoken of.

KING
It seems then that the tidings of this broil
Brake off our business for the Holy Land.

WESTMORLAND
This matched with other did, my gracious lord;   49
For more uneven and unwelcome news   50
Came from the north, and thus it did import:
On Holy Rood Day, the gallant Hotspur there,   52
Young Harry Percy, and brave Archibald,
That ever-valiant and approvèd Scot,   54
At Holmedon met, where they did spend   55
A sad and bloody hour,
As by discharge of their artillery,   57
And shape of likelihood, the news was told;   58
For he that brought them, in the very heat   59

29 **bootless** useless   31 **Of** from.   **gentle cousin** noble kinsman
33 **dear expedience** urgent expedition   34 **hot in question** being hotly
debated   35 **limits . . . charge** particulars of military responsibility
36 **athwart** at cross purposes, contrarily   37 **post** messenger.   **loaden**
heavily laden   43 **corpse** corpses   44 **transformation** mutilation
49 **other** i.e., other news   50 **uneven** disconcerting, distressing   52 **Holy
Rood Day** September 14   54 **approvèd** proved by experience
55 **Holmedon** Humbleton in Northumberland   57 **by** i.e., judging
from   58 **shape of likelihood** likely outcome   59 **them** i.e., the news

And pride of their contention did take horse,   60
Uncertain of the issue any way.

KING
Here is a dear, a true industrious friend,
Sir Walter Blunt, new lighted from his horse,
Stained with the variation of each soil
Betwixt that Holmedon and this seat of ours;
And he hath brought us smooth and welcome news.   66
The Earl of Douglas is discomfited;   67
Ten thousand bold Scots, two-and-twenty knights,
Balked in their own blood, did Sir Walter see   69
On Holmedon's plains. Of prisoners, Hotspur took
Mordake Earl of Fife and eldest son   71
To beaten Douglas, and the Earl of Atholl,
Of Murray, Angus, and Menteith.
And is not this an honorable spoil?
A gallant prize? Ha, cousin, is it not?

WESTMORLAND
In faith, it is a conquest for a prince to boast of.

KING
Yea, there thou mak'st me sad, and mak'st me sin
In envy that my lord Northumberland
Should be the father to so blest a son—
A son who is the theme of honor's tongue,
Amongst a grove the very straightest plant,   81
Who is sweet Fortune's minion and her pride,   82
Whilst I, by looking on the praise of him,
See riot and dishonor stain the brow
Of my young Harry. O, that it could be proved
That some night-tripping fairy had exchanged   86
In cradle clothes our children where they lay,
And called mine Percy, his Plantagenet!   88
Then would I have his Harry, and he mine.
But let him from my thoughts. What think you, coz,   90
Of this young Percy's pride? The prisoners
Which he in this adventure hath surprised   92

60 pride height   **66 smooth** pleasant   **67 discomfited** defeated
69 Balked heaped up in balks, or ridges   **71 Mordake** i.e., Murdoch, son
of the Earl of Albany   **81 plant** i.e., tree   **82 minion** favorite   **86 night-
tripping** i.e., moving nimbly in the night   **88 Plantagenet** (Family name
of English royalty since Henry II.)   **90 let him** let him go.   **coz** cousin,
i.e., kinsman   **92 surprised** ambushed, captured

To his own use he keeps, and sends me word   93
I shall have none but Mordake Earl of Fife.   94

WESTMORLAND
  This is his uncle's teaching, this is Worcester,
  Malevolent to you in all aspects,   96
  Which makes him prune himself and bristle up   97
  The crest of youth against your dignity.

KING
  But I have sent for him to answer this;
  And for this cause awhile we must neglect
  Our holy purpose to Jerusalem.
  Cousin, on Wednesday next our Council we
  Will hold at Windsor. So inform the lords.
  But come yourself with speed to us again,
  For more is to be said and to be done
  Than out of anger can be utterèd.

WESTMORLAND   I will, my liege.   *Exeunt.*

✦

1.2   *Enter Prince of Wales and Sir John Falstaff.*

FALSTAFF   Now, Hal, what time of day is it, lad?
PRINCE   Thou art so fat-witted with drinking of old sack,   2
  and unbuttoning thee after supper, and sleeping upon
  benches after noon, that thou hast forgotten to de-   4
  mand that truly which thou wouldst truly know. What
  a devil hast thou to do with the time of the day? Unless 6
  hours were cups of sack, and minutes capons, and
  clocks the tongues of bawds, and dials the signs of   8
  leaping houses, and the blessed sun himself a fair hot   9
  wench in flame-colored taffeta, I see no reason why   10

---

93 To ... use i.e., to collect ransom for them   **94 none but Mordake**
(Since Mordake was of royal blood, being grandson to Robert II of
Scotland, Hotspur could not claim him as his prisoner according to the
law of arms.)   **96 Malevolent, aspects** (Astrological terms.)   **97 Which
... himself** i.e., which teaching makes Hotspur preen himself (as a
falcon preens its feathers)

1.2. Location: London. An apartment of the Prince's.
2 sack a Spanish white wine   **4 forgotten** forgotten how   **6 a devil** in
the devil   **8 dials** clocks   **9 leaping houses** houses of prostitution
10 taffeta (Commonly worn by prostitutes.)

thou shouldst be so superfluous to demand the time 11
of the day.

FALSTAFF Indeed, you come near me now, Hal, for we 13
that take purses go by the moon and the seven stars, 14
and not by Phoebus, "he, that wandering knight so 15
fair." And I prithee, sweet wag, when thou art king, 16
as, God save Thy Grace—Majesty I should say, for 17
grace thou wilt have none—

PRINCE What, none?

FALSTAFF No, by my troth, not so much as will serve to 20
be prologue to an egg and butter. 21

PRINCE Well, how then? Come, roundly, roundly. 22

FALSTAFF Marry, then, sweet wag, when thou art king, 23
let not us that are squires of the night's body be called 24
thieves of the day's beauty. Let us be Diana's foresters, 25
gentlemen of the shade, minions of the moon; and let 26
men say we be men of good government, being gov- 27
erned, as the sea is, by our noble and chaste mistress
the moon, under whose countenance we steal. 29

PRINCE Thou sayest well, and it holds well too, for the 30
fortune of us that are the moon's men doth ebb and
flow like the sea, being governed, as the sea is, by the
moon. As, for proof, now: a purse of gold most reso-
lutely snatched on Monday night and most dissolutely
spent on Tuesday morning, got with swearing "Lay 35
by" and spent with crying "Bring in," now in as low 36

---

11 superfluous (1) unnecessarily concerned (2) self-indulgent   **13 you
. . . now** i.e., you've scored a point on me   **14 go by** (1) travel by the light
of (2) tell time by.   **the seven stars** the Pleiades   **15–16 Phoebus . . . fair**
(Phoebus, god of the sun, is here equated with the wandering knight of
a ballad or popular romance.)   **17 Grace** royal highness (with pun on
spiritual *grace* and also on the *grace* or blessing before a meal)
20 troth faith   **21 prologue . . . butter** i.e., grace before a brief meal
22 roundly i.e., out with it   **23 Marry** indeed. (Literally, "by the Virgin
Mary.")   **wag** joker   **24–25 let . . . beauty** i.e., let not us who are attendants on the goddess of night, members of her household, be blamed for
stealing daylight by sleeping in the daytime   **25 Diana's foresters** (An
elegant name for thieves by night; Diana is goddess of the moon and the
hunt.)   **26 minions** favorites   **27 government** (1) conduct (2) commonwealth   **29 countenance** (1) face (2) patronage, approval.   **steal** (1) move
stealthily (2) rob   **30 it holds well** the comparison is apt   **35–36 Lay by**
(A cry of highwaymen, like "Hands up!")   **36 Bring in** (An order given
to a waiter in a tavern.)

an ebb as the foot of the ladder and by and by in as ³⁷
high a flow as the ridge of the gallows. ³⁸

FALSTAFF By the Lord, thou sayst true, lad. And is not
my hostess of the tavern a most sweet wench?

PRINCE As the honey of Hybla, my old lad of the castle. ⁴¹
And is not a buff jerkin a most sweet robe of durance? ⁴²

FALSTAFF How now, how now, mad wag, what, in thy
quips and thy quiddities? What a plague have I to do ⁴⁴
with a buff jerkin?

PRINCE Why, what a pox have I to do with my hostess ⁴⁶
of the tavern?

FALSTAFF Well, thou hast called her to a reckoning many ⁴⁸
a time and oft.

PRINCE Did I ever call for thee to pay thy part?

FALSTAFF No, I'll give thee thy due, thou hast paid all
there.

PRINCE Yea, and elsewhere, so far as my coin would
stretch, and where it would not I have used my credit.

FALSTAFF Yea, and so used it that, were it not here apparent that thou art heir apparent— But I prithee,
sweet wag, shall there be gallows standing in England
when thou art king? And resolution thus fubbed as it ⁵⁸
is with the rusty curb of old Father Antic the law? Do ⁵⁹
not thou, when thou art king, hang a thief.

PRINCE No, thou shalt.

FALSTAFF Shall I? O rare! By the Lord, I'll be a brave ⁶²
judge.

PRINCE Thou judgest false already. I mean, thou shalt
have the hanging of the thieves, and so become a rare ⁶⁵
hangman.

---

37 ladder (1) pier ladder (2) gallows ladder **38 ridge** crossbar
41 Hybla (A town, famed for its honey, in Sicily near Syracuse.) **old . . .
castle** (1) a roisterer (2) the name, Sir John Oldcastle, borne by Falstaff
in the earlier version of the Henry IV plays **42 buff jerkin** a leather
jacket worn by officers of the law. **durance** (1) imprisonment (2) du-
rability, durable cloth **44 quiddities** subtleties of speech **46 pox**
syphilis. (Here, *what a pox* is used as an expletive, like "what the
devil.") **48 reckoning** settlement of the bill (with bawdy suggestion)
58 resolution courage (of a highwayman). **fubbed** cheated **59 Antic**
buffoon **62 brave** excellent **65 have . . . thieves** (1) be in charge of
hanging thieves (or protecting them from hanging) (2) hang like other
thieves. **rare** (1) rarely used (2) excellent

FALSTAFF   Well, Hal, well; and in some sort it jumps 67
with my humor as well as waiting in the court, I can 68
tell you.

PRINCE   For obtaining of suits? 70

FALSTAFF   Yea, for obtaining of suits, whereof the hangman hath no lean wardrobe. 'Sblood, I am as melan- 72
choly as a gib cat or a lugged bear. 73

PRINCE   Or an old lion, or a lover's lute.

FALSTAFF   Yea, or the drone of a Lincolnshire bagpipe.

PRINCE   What sayest thou to a hare, or the melancholy 76
of Moorditch? 77

FALSTAFF   Thou hast the most unsavory similes, and art
indeed the most comparative, rascalliest, sweet young 79
prince. But, Hal, I prithee, trouble me no more with
vanity. I would to God thou and I knew where a com- 81
modity of good names were to be bought. An old lord 82
of the Council rated me the other day in the street 83
about you, sir, but I marked him not; and yet he talked
very wisely, but I regarded him not; and yet he talked
wisely, and in the street too.

PRINCE   Thou didst well, for wisdom cries out in the 87
streets and no man regards it. 88

FALSTAFF   O, thou hast damnable iteration, and art in- 89
deed able to corrupt a saint. Thou hast done much
harm upon me, Hal, God forgive thee for it! Before I
knew thee, Hal, I knew nothing; and now am I, if a 92
man should speak truly, little better than one of the
wicked. I must give over this life, and I will give it
over. By the Lord, an I do not I am a villain. I'll be 95
damned for never a king's son in Christendom.

67–68 jumps . . . humor suits my temperament   **68 waiting in the court**
being in attendance at the royal court   **70 suits** petitions. (But Falstaff
uses the word to mean suits of clothes; clothes belonging to an executed
man were given to the executioner.)   **72 'Sblood** by his (Christ's)
blood   **73 gib cat** tomcat.   **lugged bear** bear led by a chain and baited
by dogs   **76 hare** (A proverbially melancholy animal.)   **77 Moorditch** (A
foul ditch draining Moorfields, outside London walls.)   **79 comparative**
given to abusive comparisons   **81 vanity** worldliness   **81–82 commodity**
supply   **82 names** reputations   **83 rated** chastised   **87–88 wisdom . . . it**
(An allusion to Proverbs 1:20–24.)   **89 iteration** repetition (of biblical
texts, with a neat twist)   **92 nothing** i.e., no evil   **95 an** if

PRINCE   Where shall we take a purse tomorrow, Jack?

FALSTAFF   Zounds, where thou wilt, lad, I'll make one. 98
An I do not, call me villain and baffle me. 99

PRINCE   I see a good amendment of life in thee—from
praying to purse taking.

FALSTAFF   Why, Hal, 'tis my vocation, Hal. 'Tis no sin
for a man to labor in his vocation.

Enter Poins.

Poins! Now shall we know if Gadshill have set a 104
match. O, if men were to be saved by merit, what 105
hole in hell were hot enough for him? This is the
most omnipotent villain that ever cried "Stand!" to a 107
true man. 108

PRINCE   Good morrow, Ned.

POINS   Good morrow, sweet Hal. What says Monsieur
Remorse? What says Sir John Sack and Sugar Jack?
How agrees the devil and thee about thy soul that
thou soldest him on Good Friday last for a cup of Ma-
deira and a cold capon's leg?

PRINCE   Sir John stands to his word; the devil shall have 115
his bargain, for he was never yet a breaker of proverbs. He will give the devil his due.

POINS   Then art thou damned for keeping thy word with
the devil.

PRINCE   Else he had been damned for cozening the 120
devil.

POINS   But, my lads, my lads, tomorrow morning, by
four o'clock early, at Gad's Hill, there are pilgrims 123
going to Canterbury with rich offerings and traders
riding to London with fat purses. I have vizards for 125
you all; you have horses for yourselves. Gadshill lies 126
tonight in Rochester. I have bespoke supper tomorrow 127
night in Eastcheap. We may do it as secure as sleep. If

98 Zounds by his (Christ's) wounds.   **make one** be one of the party
99 baffle publicly disgrace   **104 Gadshill** (The name of one of the
highwaymen.)   **104–105 set a match** arranged a robbery   **105 by merit**
i.e., according to their deservings rather than by God's grace
107 omnipotent i.e., unparalleled, utter   **108 true** honest   **115 stands to**
keeps   **120 Else** otherwise.   **cozening** cheating   **123 Gad's Hill** (Location near Rochester on the road from London to Canterbury; one of the
highwaymen is called Gadshill.)   **125 vizards** masks   **126 lies** lodges
127 bespoke ordered

you will go, I will stuff your purses full of crowns; if
you will not, tarry at home and be hanged.

FALSTAFF   Hear ye, Yedward, if I tarry at home and go   131
not, I'll hang you for going.   132

POINS   You will, chops?   133

FALSTAFF   Hal, wilt thou make one?

PRINCE   Who, I rob? I a thief? Not I, by my faith.

FALSTAFF   There's neither honesty, manhood, nor good
fellowship in thee, nor thou cam'st not of the blood
royal, if thou darest not stand for ten shillings.   138

PRINCE   Well then, once in my days I'll be a madcap.

FALSTAFF   Why, that's well said.

PRINCE   Well, come what will, I'll tarry at home.

FALSTAFF   By the Lord, I'll be a traitor then, when thou
art king.

PRINCE   I care not.

POINS   Sir John, I prithee leave the Prince and me alone.
I will lay him down such reasons for this adventure
that he shall go.

FALSTAFF   Well, God give thee the spirit of persuasion
and him the ears of profiting, that what thou speakest
may move and what he hears may be believed, that
the true prince may, for recreation's sake, prove a false
thief; for the poor abuses of the time want counte-   152
nance. Farewell. You shall find me in Eastcheap.   153

PRINCE   Farewell, thou latter spring! Farewell, All-   154
hallow summer!   [*Exit Falstaff.*]   155

POINS   Now, my good sweet honey lord, ride with us
tomorrow. I have a jest to execute that I cannot manage
alone. Falstaff, Peto, Bardolph, and Gadshill shall rob
those men that we have already waylaid; yourself and   159
I will not be there; and when they have the booty, if
you and I do not rob them, cut this head off from my
shoulders.

PRINCE   How shall we part with them in setting forth?

131 Yedward (Nickname for *Edward*, Poins's first name.)   132 hang you
have you hanged   133 chops i.e., fat jaws or cheeks   138 stand . . .
shillings (1) stand up and fight for money (2) be worth 10 shillings, the
value of the *royal*, the gold coin alluded to in *blood royal* (ll. 137–138)
152–153 want countenance lack encouragement and protection (from
men of rank)   154–155 All-hallow summer (Cf. "Indian summer";
Falstaff's summer or *latter spring*, i.e., his youth, has lasted to All
Saints' Day, November 1.)   159 waylaid set an ambush for

POINS   Why, we will set forth before or after them, and
appoint them a place of meeting, wherein it is at our
pleasure to fail; and then will they adventure upon the   166
exploit themselves, which they shall have no sooner
achieved but we'll set upon them.

PRINCE   Yea, but 'tis like that they will know us by our   169
horses, by our habits, and by every other appoint-   170
ment, to be ourselves.   171

POINS   Tut, our horses they shall not see—I'll tie them
in the wood; our vizards we will change after we leave
them; and, sirrah, I have cases of buckram for the   174
nonce, to immask our noted outward garments.   175

PRINCE   Yea, but I doubt they will be too hard for us.   176

POINS   Well, for two of them, I know them to be as true-
bred cowards as ever turned back; and for the third, if   178
he fight longer than he sees reason, I'll forswear arms.
The virtue of this jest will be the incomprehensible lies   180
that this same fat rogue will tell us when we meet at
supper—how thirty at least he fought with, what
wards, what blows, what extremities he endured; and   183
in the reproof of this lives the jest.   184

PRINCE   Well, I'll go with thee. Provide us all things necessary and meet me tomorrow night in Eastcheap.
There I'll sup. Farewell.

POINS   Farewell, my lord.   *Exit Poins.*

PRINCE

I know you all, and will awhile uphold
The unyoked humor of your idleness.   190
Yet herein will I imitate the sun,
Who doth permit the base contagious clouds   192
To smother up his beauty from the world,
That when he please again to be himself,   194
Being wanted, he may be more wondered at   195
By breaking through the foul and ugly mists

166 pleasure choice, discretion   **169 like** likely   **170 habits** garments
170–171 appointment accoutrement   **174 sirrah** (Usually addressed to
an inferior; here, a sign of intimacy.)   **174–175 cases . . . nonce** suits of
buckram, a stiff-finished heavily sized fabric, for the purpose
175 immask hide, disguise.   **noted** known   **176 doubt** fear.   **too hard**
too formidable   **178 turned back** turned their backs and ran away
180 incomprehensible boundless   **183 wards** parries   **184 reproof**
disproof   **190 unyoked** uncontrolled.   **idleness** frivolity   **192 contagious** noxious   **194 That** so that   **195 wanted** missed, lacked

Of vapors that did seem to strangle him.
If all the year were playing holidays,
To sport would be as tedious as to work;
But when they seldom come, they wished-for come,
And nothing pleaseth but rare accidents.   201
So when this loose behavior I throw off
And pay the debt I never promisèd,
By how much better than my word I am,
By so much shall I falsify men's hopes;   205
And like bright metal on a sullen ground,   206
My reformation, glittering o'er my fault,
Shall show more goodly and attract more eyes
Than that which hath no foil to set it off.   209
I'll so offend to make offense a skill,   210
Redeeming time when men think least I will.   *Exit.* 211

♣

1.3   *Enter the King, Northumberland, Worcester,*
Hotspur, Sir Walter Blunt, with others.

KING
My blood hath been too cold and temperate,
Unapt to stir at these indignities,   2
And you have found me, for accordingly   3
You tread upon my patience. But be sure
I will from henceforth rather be myself,   5
Mighty and to be feared, than my condition,   6
Which hath been smooth as oil, soft as young down,
And therefore lost that title of respect
Which the proud soul ne'er pays but to the proud.
WORCESTER
Our house, my sovereign liege, little deserves   10
The scourge of greatness to be used on it—   11

201 accidents events   **205 hopes** expectations   **206 sullen ground** dark
background, like a *foil.* (See l. 209.)   **209 foil** metal sheet laid contrastingly behind a jewel to set off its luster   **210 to** as to.   **skill** i.e., clever
tactic, piece of good policy   **211 Redeeming time** i.e., making amends
for lost time

1.3. Location: London. The royal court.
2 Unapt not readily disposed   **3 found me** i.e., found me so   **5 myself**
i.e., my royal self   **6 my condition** my natural (mild) disposition
10 Our house i.e., the Percy family   **11 scourge** whip

And that same greatness too which our own hands
Have holp to make so portly.   13
NORTHUMBERLAND [*To the King*]   My lord—
KING
Worcester, get thee gone, for I do see
Danger and disobedience in thine eye.
O, sir, your presence is too bold and peremptory,
And majesty might never yet endure
The moody frontier of a servant brow.   19
You have good leave to leave us. When we need   20
Your use and counsel, we shall send for you.

                                                    Exit Worcester.

[*To Northumberland.*] You were about to speak.
NORTHUMBERLAND   Yea, my good lord.
Those prisoners in Your Highness' name demanded,
Which Harry Percy here at Holmedon took,
Were, as he says, not with such strength denied   25
As is delivered to Your Majesty.   26
Either envy, therefore, or misprision   27
Is guilty of this fault, and not my son.
HOTSPUR
My liege, I did deny no prisoners.
But I remember when the fight was done,
When I was dry with rage and extreme toil,
Breathless and faint, leaning upon my sword,
Came there a certain lord, neat and trimly dressed,
Fresh as a bridegroom, and his chin new reaped   34
Showed like a stubble land at harvest home.   35
He was perfumèd like a milliner,   36
And twixt his finger and his thumb he held
A pouncet box, which ever and anon   38
He gave his nose and took 't away again,
Who therewith angry, when it next came there,   40

---

13 holp helped.   **portly** majestic, prosperous   **19 moody frontier** i.e.,
angry brow, frown. (*Frontier* literally means "outwork" or "fortifica-
tion.")   **20 good leave** full permission   **25 strength** vehemence
26 delivered reported   **27 envy** malice.   **misprision** misunderstand-
ing   **34 chin new reaped** i.e., with beard newly trimmed according to
the latest fashion, not like a soldier's beard   **35 Showed** looked.
harvest home end of harvest, fields being neat and bare   **36 milliner**
man dealing in fancy articles such as gloves and hats   **38 pouncet box**
perfume box with perforated lid   **40 Who** i.e., his nose

Took it in snuff; and still he smiled and talked,   41
And as the soldiers bore dead bodies by
He called them untaught knaves, unmannerly,
To bring a slovenly unhandsome corpse
Betwixt the wind and his nobility.
With many holiday and lady terms   46
He questioned me, amongst the rest demanded   47
My prisoners in Your Majesty's behalf.
I then, all smarting with my wounds being cold,
To be so pestered with a popinjay,   50
Out of my grief and my impatience   51
Answered neglectingly I know not what,
He should, or he should not; for he made me mad
To see him shine so brisk, and smell so sweet,
And talk so like a waiting-gentlewoman
Of guns and drums and wounds—God save the mark!—   56
And telling me the sovereignest thing on earth   57
Was parmacety for an inward bruise,   58
And that it was great pity, so it was,
This villainous saltpeter should be digged   60
Out of the bowels of the harmless earth,
Which many a good tall fellow had destroyed   62
So cowardly, and but for these vile guns
He would himself have been a soldier.
This bald unjointed chat of his, my lord,   65
I answered indirectly, as I said,   66
And I beseech you, let not his report
Come current for an accusation   68
Betwixt my love and your high majesty.

BLUNT

The circumstance considered, good my lord,
Whate'er Lord Harry Percy then had said
To such a person and in such a place,

41 Took it in snuff (1) inhaled it (2) took offense.   **still** continually
46 holiday and lady dainty and effeminate   **47 questioned** (1) conversed
with (2) put questions to   **50 popinjay** parrot   **51 grief** pain   **56 God
. . . mark** (Probably originally a formula to avert evil omen; here, an
expression of impatience.)   **57 sovereignest** most efficacious
58 parmacety spermaceti, a fatty substance taken from the head of the
sperm whale, used as a medicinal ointment   **60 saltpeter** potassium
nitrate, used to make gunpowder and also used medicinally   **62 tall**
brave   **65 bald** trivial   **66 indirectly** inattentively, offhandedly
68 Come current (1) be taken at face value (2) come rushing in

At such a time, with all the rest retold,
May reasonably die, and never rise
To do him wrong or any way impeach   75
What then he said, so he unsay it now.   76

KING

Why, yet he doth deny his prisoners,   77
But with proviso and exception,   78
That we at our own charge shall ransom straight   79
His brother-in-law, the foolish Mortimer,   80
Who, on my soul, hath willfully betrayed
The lives of those that he did lead to fight
Against that great magician, damned Glendower,
Whose daughter, as we hear, that Earl of March   84
Hath lately married. Shall our coffers then
Be emptied to redeem a traitor home?
Shall we buy treason and indent with fears   87
When they have lost and forfeited themselves?
No, on the barren mountains let him starve!
For I shall never hold that man my friend
Whose tongue shall ask me for one penny cost
To ransom home revolted Mortimer.   92

HOTSPUR   Revolted Mortimer!
He never did fall off, my sovereign liege,   94
But by the chance of war. To prove that true
Needs no more but one tongue for all those wounds,
Those mouthèd wounds, which valiantly he took,   97
When on the gentle Severn's sedgy bank,   98
In single opposition, hand to hand,
He did confound the best part of an hour   100

75 impeach discredit   **76 so** provided that   **77 yet** (emphatic) i.e., even
now.   **deny** refuse to surrender   **78 proviso and exception** (synonymous
terms)   **79 straight** straightway, at once   **80, 84 Mortimer, Earl of March**
(There were two Edmund Mortimers; Shakespeare confuses them and
combines their stories. It was the uncle [1376–1409?] who was captured
by Glendower and married Glendower's daughter; it was the nephew
[1391–1425], fifth Earl of March, who was proclaimed heir presumptive to
King Richard II after the death of his father, the fourth earl, whom Richard had named as his heir. The uncle was brother to the fourth earl and
to Hotspur's wife, Elizabeth, called Kate in this play.)   **87 indent with
fears** i.e., make a bargain or come to terms with traitors whom we have
reason to fear   **92 revolted** rebellious   **94 fall off** abandon his loyalty
97 mouthèd gaping and eloquent   **98 Severn's** (The Severn River flows
from northern Wales and western England into the Bristol Channel.)
sedgy covered with weeds   **100 confound** consume

In changing hardiment with great Glendower.   101
Three times they breathed, and three times did they
   drink,   102
Upon agreement, of swift Severn's flood,   103
Who then, affrighted with their bloody looks,   104
Ran fearfully among the trembling reeds
And hid his crisp head in the hollow bank,   106
Bloodstainèd with these valiant combatants.
Never did bare and rotten policy   108
Color her working with such deadly wounds,   109
Nor never could the noble Mortimer
Receive so many, and all willingly.
Then let not him be slandered with revolt.   112

KING
Thou dost belie him, Percy, thou dost belie him!
He never did encounter with Glendower.
I tell thee,
He durst as well have met the devil alone
As Owen Glendower for an enemy.
Art thou not ashamed? But, sirrah, henceforth
Let me not hear you speak of Mortimer.
Send me your prisoners with the speediest means,
Or you shall hear in such a kind from me   121
As will displease you. My lord Northumberland,
We license your departure with your son.
Send us your prisoners, or you will hear of it.
              Exit King [*with Blunt, and train*].

HOTSPUR
An if the devil come and roar for them   125
I will not send them. I will after straight   126
And tell him so, for I will ease my heart,
Albeit I make a hazard of my head.

NORTHUMBERLAND
What, drunk with choler? Stay and pause awhile.   129
Here comes your uncle.

    Enter Worcester.

---

101 changing hardiment exchanging blows, matching valor
102 breathed paused for breath   **103 flood** river   **104 Who** i.e., the
river   **106 crisp** curly, i.e., rippled   **108 bare** paltry.   **policy** cunning
109 Color disguise   **112 revolt** i.e., the accusation of rebellion
121 kind manner   **125 An if** if   **126 will after straight** will go after
immediately   **129 choler** anger

HOTSPUR   Speak of Mortimer?
Zounds, I will speak of him, and let my soul
Want mercy if I do not join with him!   132
Yea, on his part I'll empty all these veins,   133
And shed my dear blood drop by drop in the dust,
But I will lift the downtrod Mortimer
As high in the air as this unthankful king,
As this ingrate and cankered Bolingbroke.   137

NORTHUMBERLAND
Brother, the King hath made your nephew mad.

WORCESTER
Who struck this heat up after I was gone?

HOTSPUR
He will forsooth have all my prisoners;   140
And when I urged the ransom once again
Of my wife's brother, then his cheek looked pale,
And on my face he turned an eye of death,   143
Trembling even at the name of Mortimer.

WORCESTER
I cannot blame him. Was not he proclaimed   145
By Richard, that dead is, the next of blood?   146

NORTHUMBERLAND
He was; I heard the proclamation.
And then it was when the unhappy king—   148
Whose wrongs in us God pardon!—did set forth   149
Upon his Irish expedition;   150
From whence he, intercepted, did return   151
To be deposed and shortly murderèd.

WORCESTER
And for whose death we in the world's wide mouth
Live scandalized and foully spoken of.

HOTSPUR
But, soft, I pray you; did King Richard then   155

132 Want mercy lack mercy, be damned   **133 on his part** i.e., fighting
on Mortimer's side   **137 cankered** spoiled, malignant.   **Bolingbroke**
i.e., King Henry IV; Hotspur pointedly refuses to acknowledge his
royalty   **140 forsooth** indeed   **143 an eye of death** a fearful look
145 he i.e., Mortimer   **146 next of blood** heir to the throne
148 unhappy unfortunate   **149 in us** caused by our doings   **150 Irish
expedition** (Richard was putting down a rebellion in Ireland when
Bolingbroke returned to England from exile.)   **151 intercepted** inter-
rupted   **155 soft** i.e., wait a minute

Proclaim my brother Edmund Mortimer   156
Heir to the crown?
NORTHUMBERLAND   He did; myself did hear it.
HOTSPUR
Nay, then I cannot blame his cousin king,   158
That wished him on the barren mountains starve.
But shall it be that you that set the crown
Upon the head of this forgetful man,
And for his sake wear the detested blot
Of murderous subornation—shall it be   163
That you a world of curses undergo,
Being the agents, or base second means,   165
The cords, the ladder, or the hangman rather?
O, pardon me that I descend so low
To show the line and the predicament   168
Wherein you range under this subtle king!   169
Shall it for shame be spoken in these days,
Or fill up chronicles in time to come,
That men of your nobility and power
Did gage them both in an unjust behalf,   173
As both of you—God pardon it!—have done,
To put down Richard, that sweet lovely rose,
And plant this thorn, this canker, Bolingbroke?   176
And shall it in more shame be further spoken
That you are fooled, discarded, and shook off
By him for whom these shames ye underwent?
No! Yet time serves wherein you may redeem   180
Your banished honors and restore yourselves
Into the good thoughts of the world again;
Revenge the jeering and disdained contempt   183
Of this proud king, who studies day and night
To answer all the debt he owes to you   185
Even with the bloody payment of your deaths.
Therefore, I say—

---

156 brother i.e., brother-in-law   **158 cousin** (with a pun on *cozen*,
"cheat")   **163 murderous subornation** the suborning of or inciting to
murder   **165 second means** agents   **168 line** station, rank; also, hangman's rope.   **predicament** category; also, dangerous situation
169 range i.e., are classified   **173 gage them** engage, pledge themselves   **176 canker** (1) canker rose or dog rose, wild and unfragrant
(2) ulcer   **180 Yet** still   **183 Revenge** i.e., wherein you may revenge
yourself against.   **disdained** disdainful   **185 answer** satisfy, discharge

WORCESTER   Peace, cousin, say no more.
And now I will unclasp a secret book,
And to your quick-conceiving discontents   189
I'll read you matter deep and dangerous,
As full of peril and adventurous spirit
As to o'erwalk a current roaring loud
On the unsteadfast footing of a spear.   193
HOTSPUR
If he fall in, good night, or sink or swim!   194
Send danger from the east unto the west,
So honor cross it from the north to south,   196
And let them grapple. O, the blood more stirs
To rouse a lion than to start a hare!
NORTHUMBERLAND
Imagination of some great exploit
Drives him beyond the bounds of patience.
HOTSPUR
By heaven, methinks it were an easy leap
To pluck bright honor from the pale-faced moon,
Or dive into the bottom of the deep,
Where fathom line could never touch the ground,   204
And pluck up drownèd honor by the locks,
So he that doth redeem her thence might wear
Without corrival all her dignities;   207
But out upon this half-faced fellowship!   208
WORCESTER
He apprehends a world of figures here,   209
But not the form of what he should attend.—   210
Good cousin, give me audience for a while.
HOTSPUR
I cry you mercy.
WORCESTER   Those same noble Scots   212
That are your prisoners—

189 quick-conceiving comprehending quickly 193 spear i.e., spear laid
across a stream as a narrow bridge 194 If . . . swim i.e., such a man,
walking over a roaring stream, is doomed if he fall in, whether he sink
or swim 196 So provided that. (Also at l. 206.) 204 fathom line a
weighted line marked at fathom intervals (six feet), used for measuring
the depth of water 207 corrival rival, competitor 208 out . . . fellowship down with this paltry business of sharing glory with others
209 figures figures of the imagination, or figures of speech 210 form
essential nature. attend give attention to 212 cry you mercy beg
your pardon

HOTSPUR   I'll keep them all!
  By God, he shall not have a Scot of them,   214
  No, if a scot would save his soul, he shall not!   215
  I'll keep them, by this hand!
WORCESTER   You start away
  And lend no ear unto my purposes.
  Those prisoners you shall keep.
HOTSPUR   Nay, I will, that's flat.   218
  He said he would not ransom Mortimer,
  Forbade my tongue to speak of Mortimer,
  But I will find him when he lies asleep,
  And in his ear I'll holler "Mortimer!"
  Nay, I'll have a starling shall be taught to speak
  Nothing but "Mortimer," and give it him
  To keep his anger still in motion.   225
WORCESTER   Hear you, cousin, a word.
HOTSPUR
  All studies here I solemnly defy,   227
  Save how to gall and pinch this Bolingbroke.
  And that same sword-and-buckler Prince of Wales—   229
  But that I think his father loves him not
  And would be glad he met with some mischance—
  I would have him poisoned with a pot of ale.
WORCESTER
  Farewell, kinsman. I'll talk to you
  When you are better tempered to attend.
NORTHUMBERLAND
  Why, what a wasp-stung and impatient fool
  Art thou to break into this woman's mood,
  Tying thine ear to no tongue but thine own!
HOTSPUR
  Why, look you, I am whipped and scourged with rods,
  Nettled and stung with pismires, when I hear   239
  Of this vile politician, Bolingbroke.   240
  In Richard's time—what do you call the place?—
  A plague upon it, it is in Gloucestershire;
  'Twas where the madcap duke his uncle kept,   243

214–215 Scot . . . scot (1) Scotsman (2) trifling amount   **218 that's flat**
that's for sure   **225 still** continually   **227 defy** renounce   **229 sword-
and-buckler** (Arms improper for a prince, who should carry rapier and
dagger.)   **239 pismires** ants. (From the urinous smell of an anthill.)
240 politician deceitful schemer   **243 kept** dwelled

His uncle York; where I first bowed my knee
Unto this king of smiles, this Bolingbroke—
'Sblood, when you and he came back from Ravens-
   purgh—   246

NORTHUMBERLAND At Berkeley Castle.   247

HOTSPUR You say true.
  Why, what a candy deal of courtesy   249
  This fawning greyhound then did proffer me!
  "Look when his infant fortune came to age,"   251
  And "gentle Harry Percy," and "kind cousin"—
  O, the devil take such cozeners!—God forgive me!   253
  Good uncle, tell your tale; I have done.

WORCESTER
  Nay, if you have not, to it again;
  We will stay your leisure.

HOTSPUR   I have done, i' faith.   256

WORCESTER
  Then once more to your Scottish prisoners.
  Deliver them up without their ransom straight,   258
  And make the Douglas' son your only means   259
  For powers in Scotland, which, for divers reasons   260
  Which I shall send you written, be assured
  Will easily be granted. [*To Northumberland.*] You, my
    lord,
  Your son in Scotland being thus employed,
  Shall secretly into the bosom creep   264
  Of that same noble prelate well beloved,
  The Archbishop.

HOTSPUR Of York, is it not?

WORCESTER True, who bears hard   268
  His brother's death at Bristol, the Lord Scroop.
  I speak not this in estimation,   270
  As what I think might be, but what I know

---

246 Ravenspurgh (A port at the mouth of the River Humber in York-
shire, now covered by the sea, where Bolingbroke landed on his return
from exile.) **247 Berkeley Castle** castle near Bristol **249 candy** sug-
ared, flattering **251 Look when** when, as soon as **253 cozeners** cheats
(with pun on *cousins*) **256 stay** await **258 Deliver them up** free them
259 the Douglas' son i.e., Mordake. (See 1.1.71 and note.) **means** i.e.,
agent **260 For powers** for raising an army **264 secretly . . . creep** win
the confidence **268 bears hard** resents **270 estimation** guesswork

Is ruminated, plotted, and set down,
And only stays but to behold the face
Of that occasion that shall bring it on.

HOTSPUR
I smell it. Upon my life, it will do well.

NORTHUMBERLAND
Before the game is afoot thou still lett'st slip.   276

HOTSPUR
Why, it cannot choose but be a noble plot.   277
And then the power of Scotland and of York,   278
To join with Mortimer, ha?

WORCESTER   And so they shall.

HOTSPUR
In faith, it is exceedingly well aimed.   280

WORCESTER
And 'tis no little reason bids us speed,
To save our heads by raising of a head;   282
For, bear ourselves as even as we can,   283
The King will always think him in our debt,   284
And think we think ourselves unsatisfied,
Till he hath found a time to pay us home.   286
And see already how he doth begin
To make us strangers to his looks of love.

HOTSPUR
He does, he does. We'll be revenged on him.

WORCESTER
Cousin, farewell. No further go in this
Than I by letters shall direct your course.
When time is ripe, which will be suddenly,   292
I'll steal to Glendower and Lord Mortimer,
Where you and Douglas and our powers at once,   294
As I will fashion it, shall happily meet   295
To bear our fortunes in our own strong arms,
Which now we hold at much uncertainty.

NORTHUMBERLAND
Farewell, good brother. We shall thrive, I trust.

---

276 still lett'st slip always let loose the dogs   **277 cannot choose but be**
cannot help being   **278 power** army   **280 aimed** designed   **282 head**
army   **283 even** carefully   **284 him** himself   **286 home** fully
292 suddenly soon   **294 at once** all together   **295 happily** fortunately

HOTSPUR

    Uncle, adieu. O, let the hours be short
    Till fields and blows and groans applaud our sport!   300
                          Exeunt.

❖

---

300 fields battlefields

2.1   *Enter a Carrier with a lantern in his hand.*

FIRST CARRIER   Heigh-ho! An it be not four by the day, 1
I'll be hanged. Charles's Wain is over the new chimney, 2
and yet our horse not packed. What, hostler! 3
HOSTLER [*Within*]   Anon, anon. 4
FIRST CARRIER   I prithee, Tom, beat Cut's saddle, put a 5
few flocks in the point. Poor jade is wrung in the with- 6
ers out of all cess. 7

    Enter another Carrier.

SECOND CARRIER   Peas and beans are as dank here as a 8
dog, and that is the next way to give poor jades the 9
bots. This house is turned upside down since Robin 10
Hostler died.
FIRST CARRIER   Poor fellow never joyed since the price
of oats rose. It was the death of him.
SECOND CARRIER   I think this be the most villainous
house in all London road for fleas. I am stung like a
tench. 16
FIRST CARRIER   Like a tench? By the Mass, there is ne'er
a king Christian could be better bit than I have been 18
since the first cock. 19
SECOND CARRIER   Why, they will allow us ne'er a jordan, 20
and then we leak in your chimney, and your chamber- 21
lye breeds fleas like a loach. 22

2.1. Location: An innyard on the London–Canterbury road.
s.d. Carrier one whose trade was conveying goods, usually by pack-
horses   **1 An** if.   **by the day** in the morning   **2 Charles's Wain** i.e.,
Charlemagne's wagon; the constellation Ursa Major (the Big Dipper)
3 yet still.   **horse** horses.   **hostler** groom   **4 Anon** right away, coming
5 beat soften.   **Cut's saddle** packsaddle of the horse named *Cut*, meaning "bobtailed"   **6 flocks** tufts of wool.   **point** pommel of the saddle.
jade nag   **6–7 wrung . . . withers** chafed (by his saddle) on the ridge
between his shoulder bones   **7 cess** measure, estimate   **8 Peas and
beans** i.e., horse fodder   **8–9 dank . . . dog** i.e., damp as can be   **9 next**
nearest, quickest   **10 bots** intestinal maggots   **16 tench** a spotted fish,
whose spots may have been likened to flea bites   **18 king Christian**
Christian king, accustomed to have the best of everything   **19 first cock**
i.e., midnight   **20 jordan** chamberpot   **21 chimney** fireplace
21–22 chamber-lye urine   **22 loach** a small freshwater fish thought to
harbor parasites

FIRST CARRIER   What, hostler! Come away and be hanged! 23
Come away.

SECOND CARRIER   I have a gammon of bacon and two 25
races of ginger, to be delivered as far as Charing Cross. 26

FIRST CARRIER   God's body, the turkeys in my pannier 27
are quite starved. What, hostler! A plague on thee! Hast
thou never an eye in thy head? Canst not hear? An 29
'twere not as good deed as drink to break the pate on 30
thee, I am a very villain. Come, and be hanged! Hast 31
no faith in thee?

Enter Gadshill.

GADSHILL   Good morrow, carriers, what's o'clock?

FIRST CARRIER   I think it be two o'clock.

GADSHILL   I prithee, lend me thy lantern to see my gelding in the stable.

FIRST CARRIER   Nay, by God, soft, I know a trick worth 37
two of that, i' faith.

GADSHILL   I pray thee, lend me thine.

SECOND CARRIER   Ay, when, canst tell? Lend me thy lan- 40
tern, quoth he! Marry, I'll see thee hanged first.

GADSHILL   Sirrah carrier, what time do you mean to
come to London?

SECOND CARRIER   Time enough to go to bed with a candle, I warrant thee. Come, neighbor Mugs, we'll call
up the gentlemen. They will along with company, for 46
they have great charge.   *Exeunt [Carriers].* 47

GADSHILL   What, ho! Chamberlain! 48

Enter Chamberlain.

CHAMBERLAIN   At hand, quoth pickpurse. 49

GADSHILL   That's even as fair as—at hand, quoth the 50
chamberlain; for thou variest no more from picking of

---

23 Come away come along   **25 gammon of bacon** ham   **26 races**
roots.   **Charing Cross** a market town lying between London and Westminster   **27 pannier** basket   **29 An** if   **30–31 to break . . . thee** to give
you a blow on the head   **31 very** true   **37 soft** i.e., wait a minute
40 Ay . . . tell i.e., never   **46–47 They . . . charge** i.e., they wish to travel
in company, because they have lots of valuable cargo   **48 Chamberlain**
(Male equivalent of a chambermaid.)   **49 At . . . pickpurse** i.e., I am
right beside you, as the pickpurse said   **50 fair** good, apt

purses than giving direction doth from laboring; thou 52
layest the plot how. 53

CHAMBERLAIN Good morrow, Master Gadshill. It holds 54
current that I told you yesternight: there's a franklin in 55
the Weald of Kent hath brought three hundred marks 56
with him in gold. I heard him tell it to one of his company last night at supper—a kind of auditor, one that
hath abundance of charge too, God knows what. They
are up already, and call for eggs and butter. They will
away presently. 61

GADSHILL Sirrah, if they meet not with Saint Nicholas' 62
clerks, I'll give thee this neck. 63

CHAMBERLAIN No, I'll none of it. I pray thee, keep that 64
for the hangman, for I know thou worshipest Saint
Nicholas as truly as a man of falsehood may.

GADSHILL What talkest thou to me of the hangman? If 67
I hang, I'll make a fat pair of gallows; for if I hang, old
Sir John hangs with me, and thou knowest he is no
starveling. Tut, there are other Trojans that thou 70
dream'st not of, the which for sport's sake are content to
do the profession some grace, that would, if matters 72
should be looked into, for their own credit's sake make
all whole. I am joined with no foot-landrakers, no 74
long-staff sixpenny strikers, none of these mad mus- 75
tachio purple-hued maltworms, but with nobility and 76
tranquillity, burgomasters and great oneyers, such as 77
can hold in, such as will strike sooner than speak, and 78
speak sooner than drink, and drink sooner than pray.
And yet, zounds, I lie, for they pray continually to

52–53 thou . . . how i.e., you don't actually do the stealing, but you give
directions, like a master workman to his apprentices   **54–55 holds
current that** holds true what   **55 a franklin** a farmer owning his own
land   **56 Weald** wooded region.   **marks** coins of the value of 13 shillings 4 pence   **61 presently** immediately   **62–63 Saint Nicholas' clerks**
highwaymen. (Saint Nicholas was popularly supposed the patron of
thieves.)   **64 I'll none** I want none   **67 What** Why   **70 Trojans** i.e., slang
for "sports" or "roisterers"   **72 profession** i.e., robbery.   **grace** credit,
favor   **74 joined** associated.   **foot-landrakers** thieves who travel on
foot   **75 long-staff sixpenny strikers** robbers with long staves who
would knock down their victims for sixpence   **75–76 mustachio purple-
hued malt-worms** common drunkards with mustaches stained with
drink   **77 tranquillity** those who lead easy lives.   **oneyers** ones (?)
78 hold in keep a secret

their saint, the commonwealth, or rather not pray to
her but prey on her, for they ride up and down on
her and make her their boots.   83

CHAMBERLAIN What, the commonwealth their boots?
Will she hold out water in foul way?   85

GADSHILL She will, she will. Justice hath liquored her.   86
We steal as in a castle, cocksure. We have the receipt   87
of fern seed; we walk invisible.   88

CHAMBERLAIN Nay, by my faith, I think you are more
beholding to the night than to fern seed for your walk-   90
ing invisible.

GADSHILL Give me thy hand. Thou shalt have a share
in our purchase, as I am a true man.   93

CHAMBERLAIN Nay, rather let me have it as you are a
false thief.

GADSHILL Go to, *homo* is a common name to all men.   96
Bid the hostler bring my gelding out of the stable. Farewell, you muddy knave.   [*Exeunt separately.*] 98

❧

2.2   *Enter Prince, Poins, Peto, [and Bardolph].*

POINS Come, shelter, shelter! I have removed Falstaff's
horse, and he frets like a gummed velvet.   2

PRINCE Stand close.   [*They step aside.*] 3

Enter Falstaff.

FALSTAFF Poins! Poins, and be hanged! Poins!

PRINCE [*Coming forward*] Peace, ye fat-kidneyed rascal!
What a brawling dost thou keep!   6

---

83 boots booty (with pun on *boots*, shoes)   **85 Will . . . way** will she let
you go dry in muddy roads, i.e., will she protect you in tight places
86 liquored (1) made waterproof by oiling (2) bribed (3) made drunk
87 as in a castle i.e., in complete security.   **receipt** recipe, formula
88 of fern seed i.e., of becoming invisible (since fern seed, almost invisible itself, was popularly supposed to render its possessor invisible)
90 beholding beholden   **93 purchase** booty   **96 homo . . . men** i.e., the
Latin name for man applies to all types   **98 muddy** stupid

2.2. Location: The highway, near Gad's Hill.
2 frets chafes (with pun on another meaning of the word applying to
gummed velvet, velvet stiffened with gum and therefore liable to *fret*,
or wear)   **3 close** concealed   **6 keep** keep up

FALSTAFF   Where's Poins, Hal?

PRINCE   He is walked up to the top of the hill. I'll go
seek him.   [*He steps aside.*]

FALSTAFF   I am accursed to rob in that thief's company.
The rascal hath removed my horse and tied him I
know not where. If I travel but four foot by the square   12
further afoot, I shall break my wind. Well, I doubt not
but to die a fair death for all this, if I scape hanging for   14
killing that rogue. I have forsworn his company hourly
any time this two-and-twenty years, and yet I am be-   16
witched with the rogue's company. If the rascal have
not given me medicines to make me love him, I'll be   18
hanged; it could not be else, I have drunk medicines.
Poins! Hal! A plague upon you both! Bardolph! Peto!
I'll starve ere I'll rob a foot further. An 'twere not as
good a deed as drink to turn true man and to leave   22
these rogues, I am the veriest varlet that ever chewed
with a tooth. Eight yards of uneven ground is three-
score-and-ten miles afoot with me, and the stony-
hearted villains know it well enough. A plague upon
it when thieves cannot be true one to another! (*They
whistle.*) Whew! A plague upon you all! Give me my   28
horse, you rogues, give me my horse, and be hanged!

PRINCE [*Coming forward*]   Peace, ye fat-guts! Lie down.
Lay thine ear close to the ground and list if thou canst   31
hear the tread of travelers.

FALSTAFF   Have you any levers to lift me up again, being
down? 'Sblood, I'll not bear mine own flesh so far
afoot again for all the coin in thy father's Exchequer.
What a plague mean ye to colt me thus?   36

PRINCE   Thou liest. Thou art not colted, thou art un-
colted.

FALSTAFF   I prithee, good Prince Hal, help me to my   39
horse, good king's son.   40

---

12 square a measuring tool   **14 fair** exemplary.   **for all** despite all
16 yet still   **18 medicines** love potions   **22 turn true man** turn honest;
turn informer   **28 Whew** (Perhaps Falstaff tries to answer the whistling
he hears, or mocks it.)   **31 list** listen   **36 colt** trick, cheat. (In ll. 37–38
Prince Hal puns on the common meaning.)   **39–40 help . . . horse** help
me to find my horse. (But in l. 41, the Prince comically retorts as
though having been asked to hold the stirrup while Falstaff mounted, as
a hostler would do.)

PRINCE   Out, ye rogue! Shall I be your hostler?

FALSTAFF   Go hang thyself in thine own heir-apparent
garters! If I be ta'en, I'll peach for this. An I have not ⁴³
ballads made on you all and sung to filthy tunes, let a
cup of sack be my poison. When a jest is so forward, ⁴⁵
and afoot too! I hate it.   ⁴⁶

    Enter Gadshill.

GADSHILL   Stand.

FALSTAFF   So I do, against my will.

POINS [*Coming forward with Bardolph and Peto*]   O, 'tis
our setter. I know his voice.   ⁵⁰

BARDOLPH   What news?

GADSHILL   Case ye, case ye, on with your vizards. ⁵²
There's money of the King's coming down the hill; 'tis
going to the King's Exchequer.

FALSTAFF   You lie, ye rogue, 'tis going to the King's
Tavern.

GADSHILL   There's enough to make us all.   ⁵⁷

FALSTAFF   To be hanged.

PRINCE   Sirs, you four shall front them in the narrow ⁵⁹
lane; Ned Poins and I will walk lower. If they scape
from your encounter, then they light on us.

PETO   How many be there of them?

GADSHILL   Some eight or ten.

FALSTAFF   Zounds, will they not rob us?

PRINCE   What, a coward, Sir John Paunch?

FALSTAFF   Indeed, I am not John of Gaunt, your grand- ⁶⁶
father, but yet no coward, Hal.

PRINCE   Well, we leave that to the proof.   ⁶⁸

POINS   Sirrah Jack, thy horse stands behind the hedge.
When thou need'st him, there thou shalt find him.
Farewell, and stand fast.

FALSTAFF   Now cannot I strike him, if I should be ⁷²
hanged.   ⁷³

---

43 peach inform on you.   **An** if   **45 so forward** (1) so far advanced
(referring to the robbery plot) (2) so presumptuous (referring to the joke
played on him)   **46 afoot** (1) in progress (2) on foot, i.e., not on horse-
back   **50 setter** arranger of the robbery. (See 1.2.104–105 and note.)
52 Case ye put on your masks   **57 make us all** make our fortunes
59 front confront   **66 Gaunt** i.e., Ghent (but punning on *gaunt*, thin)
68 proof test   **72–73 Now . . . hanged** (Falstaff wishes he could hit
Poins, who is too quick for him.)

PRINCE [*To Poins*] Ned, where are our disguises?
POINS [*To Prince*] Here, hard by. Stand close.
                              [*Exeunt Prince and Poins.*]
FALSTAFF Now, my masters, happy man be his dole,   76
   say I. Every man to his business.

   Enter the Travelers.

FIRST TRAVELER Come, neighbor. The boy shall lead our
   horses down the hill; we'll walk afoot awhile and ease
   our legs.
THIEVES Stand!
TRAVELERS Jesus bless us!
FALSTAFF Strike! Down with them! Cut the villains'
   throats! Ah, whoreson caterpillars, bacon-fed knaves!   84
   They hate us youth. Down with them, fleece them!
TRAVELERS O, we are undone, both we and ours for-
   ever!
FALSTAFF Hang ye, gorbellied knaves, are ye undone?   88
   No, ye fat chuffs, I would your store were here! On,   89
   bacons, on! What, ye knaves, young men must live.   90
   You are grandjurors, are ye? We'll jure ye, 'faith.   91
              Here they rob them and bind them. Exeunt.

   Enter the Prince and Poins [in buckram].

PRINCE The thieves have bound the true men. Now
   could thou and I rob the thieves and go merrily to London, it would be argument for a week, laughter for a   94
   month, and a good jest forever.
POINS Stand close. I hear them coming.
                              [*They stand aside.*]

   Enter the thieves again.

FALSTAFF Come, my masters, let us share, and then to
   horse before day. An the Prince and Poins be not two
   arrant cowards, there's no equity stirring. There's no   99

76 happy . . . dole may happiness be every man's portion or lot
84 whoreson i.e., scurvy, abominable. **caterpillars** i.e., parasites.
bacon-fed i.e., well-fed **88 gorbellied** big-bellied **89 chuffs** churls, rich
but miserly. **store** total wealth **90 bacons** fat men **91 grandjurors**
i.e., men of wealth, able to serve on juries **94 argument** a subject for
conversation **99 arrant** notorious, unmitigated. **equity** judgment,
discernment

more valor in that Poins than in a wild duck.

> [*The thieves begin to share the booty.*]

PRINCE   Your money!

POINS   Villains!

> *As they are sharing, the Prince and Poins set*
> *upon them. They all run away, and Falstaff,*
> *after a blow or two, runs away too,*
> *leaving the booty behind them.*

PRINCE

Got with much ease. Now merrily to horse.
The thieves are all scattered and possessed with fear
So strongly that they dare not meet each other;
Each takes his fellow for an officer.
Away, good Ned. Falstaff sweats to death
And lards the lean earth as he walks along.   108
Were 't not for laughing, I should pity him.

POINS   How the fat rogue roared!   *Exeunt.*

✚

2.3   *Enter Hotspur, solus, reading a letter.*

HOTSPUR   "But, for mine own part, my lord, I could be
well contented to be there, in respect of the love I bear
your house." He could be contented; why is he not,   3
then? In respect of the love he bears our house! He
shows in this, he loves his own barn better than he   5
loves our house. Let me see some more. "The purpose
you undertake is dangerous"—why, that's certain.
'Tis dangerous to take a cold, to sleep, to drink; but I
tell you, my lord fool, out of this nettle, danger, we
pluck this flower, safety. "The purpose you undertake
is dangerous, the friends you have named uncertain,
the time itself unsorted, and your whole plot too light   12
for the counterpoise of so great an opposition." Say   13
you so, say you so? I say unto you again, you are a

---

108 lards drips fat, bastes

**2.3. Location: Hotspur's estate (identified historically as Warkworth
Castle in Northumberland).**

s.d. solus alone   **3 house** family   **5 barn** (Hotspur refers derisively to
the writer's residence, taking *house*, l. 3, in its literal sense.)   **12 unsorted** unsuitable   **13 for . . . of** to counterbalance

shallow, cowardly hind, and you lie. What a lack- 15
brain is this! By the Lord, our plot is a good plot as
ever was laid, our friends true and constant; a good
plot, good friends, and full of expectation; an excellent 18
plot, very good friends. What a frosty-spirited rogue is
this! Why, my lord of York commends the plot and 20
the general course of the action. Zounds, an I were 21
now by this rascal, I could brain him with his lady's
fan. Is there not my father, my uncle, and myself? Lord
Edmund Mortimer, my lord of York, and Owen Glendower? Is there not besides the Douglas? Have I not
all their letters to meet me in arms by the ninth of the
next month, and are they not some of them set forward already? What a pagan rascal is this, an infidel! 28
Ha, you shall see now in very sincerity of fear and
cold heart will he to the King and lay open all our
proceedings. O, I could divide myself and go to buf- 31
fets for moving such a dish of skim milk with so hon- 32
orable an action! Hang him, let him tell the King, we
are prepared. I will set forward tonight.

Enter his Lady.

How now, Kate? I must leave you within these two
hours.

LADY PERCY
O, my good lord, why are you thus alone?
For what offense have I this fortnight been
A banished woman from my Harry's bed?
Tell me, sweet lord, what is 't that takes from thee
Thy stomach, pleasure, and thy golden sleep?   41
Why dost thou bend thine eyes upon the earth
And start so often when thou sitt'st alone?
Why hast thou lost the fresh blood in thy cheeks
And given my treasures and my rights of thee   45
To thick-eyed musing and curst melancholy?   46

---

15 hind menial, peasant **18 expectation** promise **20 lord of York** i.e.,
Archbishop Scroop. (Also in l. 24.) **21 an** if **28 pagan** unbelieving
31–32 divide . . . buffets i.e., fight with myself **32 moving** urging
41 stomach appetite **45 And . . . thee** i.e., and given what I treasure in
you and have a right, as wife, to share **46 thick-eyed** dull-sighted,
vacant, abstracted. **curst** ill-tempered

In thy faint slumbers I by thee have watched   47
And heard thee murmur tales of iron wars,
Speak terms of manage to thy bounding steed,   49
Cry, "Courage! To the field!" And thou hast talked
Of sallies and retires, of trenches, tents,   51
Of palisadoes, frontiers, parapets,   52
Of basilisks, of cannon, culverin,   53
Of prisoners' ransom, and of soldiers slain,
And all the currents of a heady fight.   55
Thy spirit within thee hath been so at war,
And thus hath so bestirred thee in thy sleep,
That beads of sweat have stood upon thy brow
Like bubbles in a late-disturbèd stream,   59
And in thy face strange motions have appeared,
Such as we see when men restrain their breath
On some great sudden hest. O, what portents are these?   62
Some heavy business hath my lord in hand,   63
And I must know it, else he loves me not.

HOTSPUR
What, ho!

          [*Enter a Servant.*]

          Is Gilliams with the packet gone?
SERVANT   He is, my lord, an hour ago.
HOTSPUR
Hath Butler brought those horses from the sheriff?
SERVANT
One horse, my lord, he brought even now.   68
HOTSPUR
What horse? Roan, a crop-ear, is it not?
SERVANT
It is, my lord.
HOTSPUR   That roan shall be my throne.
Well, I will back him straight. O, *Esperance*!   71
Bid Butler lead him forth into the park.

          [*Exit Servant.*]

---

47 faint i.e., restless.   **watched** lain awake   **49 manage** horsemanship
51 retires retreats   **52 palisadoes** stakes set in the ground for defense.
frontiers outworks, ramparts   **53 basilisks** large cannon.   **culverin** long
cannon   **55 heady** headlong   **59 late-disturbèd** recently stirred up
62 hest command   **63 heavy** weighty; sorrowful   **68 even** just   **71 back**
mount.   **Esperance** hope. (The motto of the Percy family.)

LADY PERCY   But hear you, my lord.

HOTSPUR   What sayst thou, my lady?

LADY PERCY   What is it carries you away?

HOTSPUR   Why, my horse, my love, my horse.

LADY PERCY   Out, you mad-headed ape!
A weasel hath not such a deal of spleen   78
As you are tossed with. In faith,   79
I'll know your business, Harry, that I will.
I fear my brother Mortimer doth stir
About his title, and hath sent for you   82
To line his enterprise; but if you go—   83

HOTSPUR
So far afoot, I shall be weary, love.

LADY PERCY
Come, come, you paraquito, answer me   85
Directly unto this question that I ask.
In faith, I'll break thy little finger, Harry,
An if thou wilt not tell me all things true.   88

HOTSPUR   Away,
Away, you trifler! Love? I love thee not;
I care not for thee, Kate. This is no world
To play with mammets and to tilt with lips.   91
We must have bloody noses and cracked crowns,   92
And pass them current too. Gods me, my horse!   93
What sayst thou, Kate? What wouldst thou have with
        me?

LADY PERCY
Do you not love me? Do you not, indeed?
Well, do not then, for since you love me not
I will not love myself. Do you not love me?
Nay, tell me if you speak in jest or no.

HOTSPUR   Come, wilt thou see me ride?
And when I am a-horseback I will swear
I love thee infinitely. But hark you, Kate,
I must not have you henceforth question me

---

78 spleen (The spleen was thought to be the source of impulsive and irritable behavior.)   **79 tossed** tossed about, agitated   **82 title** claim to the throne   **83 line** strengthen   **85 paraquito** little parrot. (A term of endearment.)   **88 An if** if   **91 mammets** dolls (with a quibble on the Latin *mamma* meaning "breast")   **92 crowns** (1) heads (2) coins worth 5 shillings. (Cracked coins would not "pass current," as Hotspur jokes in the next line.)   **93 Gods me** God save me

Whither I go, nor reason whereabout.   103
Whither I must, I must; and, to conclude,
This evening must I leave you, gentle Kate.
I know you wise, but yet no farther wise
Than Harry Percy's wife; constant you are,
But yet a woman; and for secrecy,
No lady closer, for I well believe   109
Thou wilt not utter what thou dost not know,
And so far will I trust thee, gentle Kate.

LADY PERCY   How, so far?

HOTSPUR
Not an inch further. But hark you, Kate:
Whither I go, thither shall you go too.
Today will I set forth, tomorrow you.
Will this content you, Kate?

LADY PERCY   It must of force.   *Exeunt.* 116

✣

2.4   *Enter Prince and Poins.*

PRINCE   Ned, prithee, come out of that fat room, and   1
lend me thy hand to laugh a little.

POINS   Where hast been, Hal?

PRINCE   With three or four loggerheads amongst three   4
or four score hogsheads. I have sounded the very bass   5
string of humility. Sirrah, I am sworn brother to a
leash of drawers, and can call them all by their Christian   7
names, as Tom, Dick, and Francis. They take it already   8
upon their salvation that, though I be but Prince of   9
Wales, yet I am the king of courtesy, and tell me flatly
I am no proud Jack like Falstaff, but a Corinthian, a lad   11
of mettle, a good boy—by the Lord, so they call me!—

---

103 reason whereabout discuss about what   **109 closer** more close-
mouthed   **116 of force** perforce, of necessity

**2.4. Location: A tavern in Eastcheap, London, usually identified as the
Boar's Head. Some tavern furniture, including stools, is provided onstage.**
1 fat stuffy; or, a vat room   **4 loggerheads** blockheads   **5 bass** (with a
pun on *base*)   **7 leash of drawers** i.e., three waiters   **8–9 take . . . salvation** already maintain it as they hope to be saved   **11 Jack** (1) Jack
Falstaff (2) fellow.   **Corinthian** i.e., gay blade, good sport. (Corinth was
reputed to be licentious.)

and when I am King of England I shall command all
the good lads in Eastcheap. They call drinking deep,   14
"dyeing scarlet"; and when you breathe in your water-   15
ing they cry "hem!" and bid you "play it off." To con-   16
clude, I am so good a proficient in one quarter of an
hour that I can drink with any tinker in his own language during my life. I tell thee, Ned, thou hast lost
much honor that thou wert not with me in this action.
But, sweet Ned—to sweeten which name of Ned, I
give thee this pennyworth of sugar, clapped even now   22
into my hand by an underskinker, one that never   23
spake other English in his life than "Eight shillings
and sixpence," and "You are welcome," with this
shrill addition, "Anon, anon, sir! Score a pint of bas-   26
tard in the Half-Moon," or so. But, Ned, to drive away   27
the time till Falstaff come, I prithee do thou stand in
some by-room while I question my puny drawer to   29
what end he gave me the sugar; and do thou never
leave calling "Francis," that his tale to me may be
nothing but "Anon." Step aside, and I'll show thee a
precedent.   [*Exit Poins.*]   33

POINS [*Within*]   Francis!
PRINCE   Thou art perfect.
POINS [*Within*]   Francis!

    Enter [Francis, a] drawer.

FRANCIS   Anon, anon, sir.—Look down into the Pomgar-   37
net, Ralph.   38
PRINCE   Come hither, Francis.
FRANCIS   My lord?
PRINCE   How long hast thou to serve, Francis?   41
FRANCIS   Forsooth, five years, and as much as to—
POINS [*Within*]   Francis!

14–15 They . . . scarlet (Either because excessive drinking causes a red
complexion or because urine, produced by *drinking deep*, was sometimes used for fixing dyes.)   **15–16 breathe . . . watering** pause for
breath in your drinking   **16 play it off** drink it up   **22 sugar** (Used to
sweeten wine.)   **23 underskinker** assistant to a waiter or bartender
26 Anon right away, coming.   **Score** charge   **26–27 bastard** (A sweet
Spanish wine.)   **27 Half-Moon** (The name of a room in the inn.)   **29 by-
room** side-room.   **puny** inexperienced, raw.   **drawer** tapster, one who
draws liquor   **33 precedent** example   **37–38 Pomgarnet** Pomegranate.
(Another room in the inn.)   **41 serve** i.e., serve out your apprenticeship

FRANCIS Anon, anon, sir.

PRINCE Five year! By 'r Lady, a long lease for the clink- 45
ing of pewter. But Francis, darest thou be so valiant
as to play the coward with thy indenture and show it 47
a fair pair of heels and run from it?

FRANCIS O Lord, sir, I'll be sworn upon all the books in 49
England, I could find in my heart—

POINS [*Within*] Francis!

FRANCIS Anon, sir.

PRINCE How old art thou, Francis?

FRANCIS Let me see, about Michaelmas next I shall 54
be—

POINS [*Within*] Francis!

FRANCIS Anon, sir. Pray, stay a little, my lord.

PRINCE Nay, but hark you, Francis: for the sugar thou
gavest me, 'twas a pennyworth, was 't not?

FRANCIS O Lord, I would it had been two!

PRINCE I will give thee for it a thousand pound. Ask me
when thou wilt, and thou shalt have it.

POINS [*Within*] Francis!

FRANCIS Anon, anon.

PRINCE Anon, Francis? No, Francis; but tomorrow,
Francis, or, Francis, o' Thursday, or indeed, Francis,
when thou wilt. But, Francis—

FRANCIS My lord?

PRINCE Wilt thou rob this leathern-jerkin, crystal- 69
button, not-pated, agate-ring, puke-stocking, caddis- 70
garter, smooth-tongue, Spanish-pouch— 71

FRANCIS O Lord, sir, who do you mean?

PRINCE Why, then, your brown bastard is your only 73
drink; for look you, Francis, your white canvas dou- 74
blet will sully. In Barbary, sir, it cannot come to so 75
much. 76

---

45 By 'r Lady by Our Lady   **47 indenture** contract of apprenticeship
49 books i.e., Bibles   **54 Michaelmas** September 29   **69–71 Wilt . . .
Spanish-pouch** i.e., will you rob your master of your services by running
away, he who is characterized by a leather jacket, transparent buttons,
cropped hair, a ring with small figures in an agate stone for a seal, dark
woolen stockings, worsted garters, an ingratiating flattering manner of
speech, a pouch of Spanish leather   **73–76 Why . . . much** (The Prince
talks seeming nonsense in order to bewilder Francis; but he also implies that Francis should stick to his trade, since he will not cut much
of a figure in the world.)   **75 it** i.e., sugar

FRANCIS What, sir?
POINS [*Within*] Francis!
PRINCE Away, you rogue! Dost thou not hear them call?
          *Here they both call him; the drawer stands
              amazed, not knowing which way to go.*

     Enter Vintner.

VINTNER What stand'st thou still and hear'st such a 80
calling? Look to the guests within. [*Exit Francis.*] My
lord, old Sir John, with half a dozen more, are at the
door. Shall I let them in?
PRINCE Let them alone awhile, and then open the door.
[*Exit Vintner.*] Poins!

     Enter Poins.

POINS Anon, anon, sir.
PRINCE Sirrah, Falstaff and the rest of the thieves are at
the door. Shall we be merry?
POINS As merry as crickets, my lad. But hark ye, what
cunning match have you made with this jest of the 90
drawer? Come, what's the issue? 91
PRINCE I am now of all humors that have showed them- 92
selves humors since the old days of Goodman Adam to 93
the pupil age of this present twelve o'clock at mid- 94
night. 95

     [*Enter Francis, hurrying across the stage with
     wine.*]

What's o'clock, Francis?
FRANCIS Anon, anon, sir.   [*Exit.*]
PRINCE That ever this fellow should have fewer words
than a parrot, and yet the son of a woman! His indus-
try is upstairs and downstairs, his eloquence the parcel 100
of a reckoning. I am not yet of Percy's mind, the Hot- 101
spur of the north, he that kills me some six or seven 102
dozen of Scots at a breakfast, washes his hands, and
says to his wife, "Fie upon this quiet life! I want

80 What why   **90 match** game, contest   **91 issue** outcome, point
92–95 I . . . midnight i.e., I'm now in a mood for anything that has
happened in the whole history of the world   **93 Goodman** (Title for a
farmer.)   **94 pupil** youthful   **100–101 parcel . . . reckoning** items of a
bill   **102 kills me** i.e., kills. (*Me* is used colloquially.)

work." "O my sweet Harry," says she, "how many
hast thou killed today?" "Give my roan horse a
drench," says he, and answers, "Some fourteen," an   107
hour after, "a trifle, a trifle." I prithee, call in Falstaff.
I'll play Percy, and that damned brawn shall play Dame   109
Mortimer his wife. "Rivo!" says the drunkard. Call in   110
ribs, call in tallow.   111

Enter Falstaff, [Gadshill, Bardolph, and Peto;
Francis following with wine].

POINS   Welcome, Jack. Where hast thou been?

FALSTAFF   A plague of all cowards, I say, and a ven-   113
geance too! Marry and amen! Give me a cup of sack,
boy. Ere I lead this life long, I'll sew netherstocks, and   115
mend them and foot them too. A plague of all cow-   116
ards! Give me a cup of sack, rogue. Is there no virtue
extant?   *He drinketh.*

PRINCE   Didst thou never see Titan kiss a dish of butter,   119
pitiful-hearted Titan, that melted at the sweet tale of   120
the sun's? If thou didst, then behold that compound.   121

FALSTAFF   You rogue, here's lime in this sack too. There   122
is nothing but roguery to be found in villainous man,
yet a coward is worse than a cup of sack with lime in
it. A villainous coward! Go thy ways, old Jack, die
when thou wilt; if manhood, good manhood, be not
forgot upon the face of the earth, then am I a shotten   127
herring. There lives not three good men unhanged in   128
England, and one of them is fat and grows old, God
help the while! A bad world, I say. I would I were a   130
weaver; I could sing psalms or anything. A plague of   131
all cowards, I say still.

PRINCE   How now, woolsack, what mutter you?   133

---

107 drench dose of medicine.   **says he** i.e., he tells a servant
109 brawn fat boar   **110 Rivo** (An exclamation of uncertain meaning,
but related to drinking.)   **111 ribs** rib roast.   **tallow** fat drippings
113 of on   **115 netherstocks** stockings (the sewing or mending of which
is a menial occupation)   **116 foot** make a new foot for   **119 Titan** i.e.,
the sun   **120 that** i.e., the butter   **121 compound** melting butter, i.e.,
Falstaff   **122 lime in this sack** i.e., lime added to make the wine spar-
kle   **127–128 shotten herring** a herring that has cast its roe and is
consequently thin   **130 the while** i.e., in these bad times   **131 weaver**
(Many psalm-singing Protestant immigrants from the Low Countries
were weavers.)   **133 woolsack** bale of wool

FALSTAFF· A king's son! If I do not beat thee out of thy
kingdom with a dagger of lath, and drive all thy sub-   135
jects afore thee like a flock of wild geese, I'll never wear
hair on my face more. You, Prince of Wales!

PRINCE Why, you whoreson round man, what's the
matter?

FALSTAFF Are not you a coward? Answer me to that.
And Poins there?

POINS Zounds, ye fat paunch, an ye call me coward, by   142
the Lord, I'll stab thee.

FALSTAFF I call thee coward? I'll see thee damned ere I
call thee coward, but I would give a thousand pound
I could run as fast as thou canst. You are straight
enough in the shoulders; you care not who sees your
back. Call you that backing of your friends? A plague
upon such backing! Give me them that will face me.
Give me a cup of sack. I am a rogue if I drunk today.

PRINCE O villain, thy lips are scarce wiped since thou
drunk'st last.

FALSTAFF All is one for that. (*He drinketh.*) A plague of   153
all cowards, still say I.

PRINCE What's the matter?

FALSTAFF What's the matter? There be four of us here
have ta'en a thousand pound this day morning.

PRINCE Where is it, Jack, where is it?

FALSTAFF Where is it? Taken from us it is. A hundred
upon poor four of us.

PRINCE What, a hundred, man?

FALSTAFF I am a rogue if I were not at half-sword with   162
a dozen of them two hours together. I have scaped by   163
miracle. I am eight times thrust through the doublet,   164
four through the hose, my buckler cut through and   165
through, my sword hacked like a handsaw—*ecce sig-*   166
num! I never dealt better since I was a man. All would   167
not do. A plague of all cowards! Let them speak. If   168

135 dagger of lath (The Vice, a stock comic figure in morality plays, was
so armed.)   **142 an** if   **153 All . . . that** i.e., no matter   **162 at half-
sword** fighting at close quarters   **163 scaped** escaped   **164 doublet**
Elizabethan upper garment like a jacket   **165 hose** close-fitting
breeches.   **buckler** shield   **166–167 ecce signum** behold the proof.
(Familiar words from the Mass.)   **167–168 All . . . do** i.e., all that I did
was of no use

they speak more or less than truth, they are villains
and the sons of darkness.

PRINCE   Speak, sirs, how was it?

GADSHILL   We four set upon some dozen—

FALSTAFF   Sixteen at least, my lord.

GADSHILL   And bound them.

PETO   No, no, they were not bound.

FALSTAFF   You rogue, they were bound, every man of
them, or I am a Jew else, an Hebrew Jew.

GADSHILL   As we were sharing, some six or seven fresh
men set upon us—

FALSTAFF   And unbound the rest, and then come in the
other.   181

PRINCE   What, fought you with them all?

FALSTAFF   All? I know not what you call all, but if I
fought not with fifty of them I am a bunch of radish.
If there were not two- or three-and-fifty upon poor old
Jack, then am I no two-legged creature.

PRINCE   Pray God you have not murdered some of them.

FALSTAFF   Nay, that's past praying for. I have peppered   188
two of them. Two I am sure I have paid, two rogues
in buckram suits. I tell thee what, Hal, if I tell thee a
lie, spit in my face, call me horse. Thou knowest my
old ward. Here I lay, and thus I bore my point. [He   192
demonstrates his stance.] Four rogues in buckram let
drive at me—

PRINCE   What, four? Thou saidst but two even now.   195

FALSTAFF   Four, Hal, I told thee four.

POINS   Ay, ay, he said four.

FALSTAFF   These four came all afront and mainly thrust   198
at me. I made me no more ado but took all their seven   199
points in my target, thus.   200

PRINCE   Seven? Why, there were but four even now.

FALSTAFF   In buckram?

POINS   Ay, four, in buckram suits.

FALSTAFF   Seven, by these hilts, or I am a villain else.   204

---

181 other others   **188 peppered** i.e., killed   **192 ward** defensive stance,
parry.   **lay** stood   **195 even** just   **198 afront** abreast.   **mainly** power-
fully   **199 made me** i.e., made. (*Me* is used colloquially.)   **200 target**
shield   **204 by these hilts** by my sword hilt.   **villain** i.e., no gentleman

PRINCE [*Aside to Poins*] Prithee, let him alone. We shall
have more anon.

FALSTAFF Dost thou hear me, Hal?

PRINCE Ay, and mark thee too, Jack.   208

FALSTAFF Do so, for it is worth the listening to. These
nine in buckram that I told thee of—

PRINCE So, two more already.

FALSTAFF Their points being broken—   212

POINS Down fell their hose.

FALSTAFF Began to give me ground; but I followed me   214
close, came in foot and hand; and with a thought   215
seven of the eleven I paid.

PRINCE O monstrous! Eleven buckram men grown out
of two!

FALSTAFF But, as the devil would have it, three misbe-
gotten knaves in Kendal green came at my back and   220
let drive at me, for it was so dark, Hal, that thou
couldst not see thy hand.

PRINCE These lies are like their father that begets them,
gross as a mountain, open, palpable. Why, thou clay-
brained guts, thou knotty-pated fool, thou whoreson,   225
obscene, greasy tallow-keech—   226

FALSTAFF What, art thou mad? Art thou mad? Is not the
truth the truth?

PRINCE Why, how couldst thou know these men in
Kendal green when it was so dark thou couldst not
see thy hand? Come, tell us your reason. What sayest
thou to this?

POINS Come, your reason, Jack, your reason.

FALSTAFF What, upon compulsion? Zounds, an I were
at the strappado, or all the racks in the world, I would   235
not tell you on compulsion. Give you a reason on compulsion? If reasons were as plentiful as blackberries, I   237
would give no man a reason upon compulsion, I.

PRINCE I'll be no longer guilty of this sin. This sanguine   239

---

208 mark (1) pay heed (2) keep count   **212 points** sword points. (But
Poins puns on the sense of laces by which the hose were attached to the
doublet.)   **214 followed me** i.e., followed   **215 with a thought** quick as a
thought   **220 Kendal** a town known for its textiles   **225 knotty-pated**
thickheaded   **226 tallow-keech** lump of tallow   **235 strappado** a kind of
torture   **237 reasons . . . blackberries** (Falstaff puns on *raisins*, pro-
nounced nearly like *reasons*.)   **239 sanguine** ruddy

coward, this bed-presser, this horse-backbreaker, this huge hill of flesh—

FALSTAFF 'Sblood, you starveling, you eelskin, you dried neat's tongue, you bull's pizzle, you stockfish! 243 O, for breath to utter what is like thee! You tailor's yard, you sheath, you bowcase, you vile standing 245 tuck— 246

PRINCE Well, breathe awhile, and then to it again, and when thou hast tired thyself in base comparisons, hear me speak but this.

POINS Mark, Jack.

PRINCE We two saw you four set on four and bound them, and were masters of their wealth. Mark now how a plain tale shall put you down. Then did we two set on you four, and, with a word, outfaced you from 254 your prize, and have it, yea, and can show it you here in the house. And, Falstaff, you carried your guts away as nimbly, with as quick dexterity, and roared for mercy, and still run and roared, as ever I heard bull calf. What a slave art thou, to hack thy sword as thou hast done, and then say it was in fight! What trick, what device, what starting-hole canst thou now find 261 out to hide thee from this open and apparent shame?

POINS Come, let's hear, Jack. What trick hast thou now?

FALSTAFF By the Lord, I knew ye as well as he that made ye. Why, hear you, my masters, was it for me to kill the heir apparent? Should I turn upon the true prince? Why, thou knowest I am as valiant as Hercules, but beware instinct. The lion will not touch the true prince. Instinct is a great matter. I was now a coward on instinct. I shall think the better of myself and thee during my life—I for a valiant lion, and thou for a true prince. But by the Lord, lads, I am glad you have the money. Hostess, clap to the doors! Watch to- 273 night, pray tomorrow. Gallants, lads, boys, hearts of 274 gold, all the titles of good fellowship come to you!

---

243 neat's ox's.   **pizzle** penis.   **stockfish** dried cod   **245 yard** yard-stick.   **standing** standing on its point, or no longer pliant   **246 tuck** rapier   **254 with a word** in a word.   **outfaced** frightened   **261 starting-hole** point of shelter (like a rabbit's hole)   **273 Watch** stay awake. (See Matthew 26:41.)   **274 pray** (1) pray to God (2) prey

What, shall we be merry? Shall we have a play extempore?

PRINCE   Content; and the argument shall be thy running 278
away.

FALSTAFF   Ah, no more of that, Hal, an thou lovest me!

Enter Hostess.

HOSTESS   O Jesu, my lord the Prince!

PRINCE   How now, my lady the hostess, what sayst
thou to me?

HOSTESS   Marry, my lord, there is a nobleman of the
court at door would speak with you. He says he comes
from your father.

PRINCE   Give him as much as will make him a royal 287
man and send him back again to my mother.   288

FALSTAFF   What manner of man is he?

HOSTESS   An old man.

FALSTAFF   What doth Gravity out of his bed at midnight? 291
Shall I give him his answer?

PRINCE   Prithee, do, Jack.

FALSTAFF   Faith, and I'll send him packing.   *Exit.*

PRINCE   Now, sirs. By 'r Lady, you fought fair; so did
you, Peto; so did you, Bardolph. You are lions too,
you ran away upon instinct, you will not touch the
true prince; no, fie!

BARDOLPH   Faith, I ran when I saw others run.

PRINCE   Faith, tell me now in earnest, how came Falstaff's sword so hacked?

PETO   Why, he hacked it with his dagger, and said he
would swear truth out of England but he would make 303
you believe it was done in fight, and persuaded us to
do the like.

BARDOLPH   Yea, and to tickle our noses with spear grass
to make them bleed, and then to beslubber our gar- 307
ments with it and swear it was the blood of true men.
I did that I did not this seven year before: I blushed to 309
hear his monstrous devices.

---

278 argument plot of the play   **287–288 Give . . . man** (Hal puns on the
value of coins: a *noble* was worth 6 shillings 8 pence, a *royal* 10 shillings.)   **291 What doth** why is   **303 but he would** if he did not
307 beslubber smear, cover   **309 that** something

PRINCE O villain, thou stolest a cup of sack eighteen
years ago and wert taken with the manner, and ever 312
since thou hast blushed extempore. Thou hadst fire 313
and sword on thy side, and yet thou rann'st away.
What instinct hadst thou for it?

BARDOLPH My lord, do you see these meteors? Do you 316
behold these exhalations? [*Pointing to his own face.*] 317

PRINCE I do.

BARDOLPH What think you they portend?   319

PRINCE Hot livers and cold purses.   320

BARDOLPH Choler, my lord, if rightly taken.   321

PRINCE No, if rightly taken, halter.   322

   Enter Falstaff.

Here comes lean Jack, here comes bare-bone. How
now, my sweet creature of bombast? How long is 't 324
ago, Jack, since thou sawest thine own knee?

FALSTAFF My own knee? When I was about thy years,
Hal, I was not an eagle's talon in the waist; I could
have crept into any alderman's thumb ring. A plague
of sighing and grief! It blows a man up like a bladder.
There's villainous news abroad. Here was Sir John
Bracy from your father. You must to the court in the
morning. That same mad fellow of the north, Percy,
and he of Wales that gave Amamon the bastinado and 333
made Lucifer cuckold and swore the devil his true 334
liegeman upon the cross of a Welsh hook—what a 335
plague call you him?

312 taken . . . manner caught with the goods   **313 extempore** with no
preparation or provocation (since drinking has left his face permanently
red).   **fire** i.e., a red nose and complexion caused by heavy drinking
316, 317 meteors, exhalations i.e., the red blotches on Bardolph's face
319 portend signify. (Continues the metaphor of astrological influence
begun in *meteors* and *exhalations*.)   **320 Hot . . . purses** i.e., livers
inflamed by drink and purses made empty by spending   **321 Choler**
a choleric or combative temperament.   **taken** understood. (But
the Prince, in his next speech, uses the word to mean "arrested.")
322 halter hangman's noose. (The Prince plays on Bardolph's *choler,*
which he takes as *collar.*)   **324 bombast** (1) cotton padding (2) fustian
speech   **333 Amamon** (The name of a demon.)   **bastinado** beating on
the soles of the feet   **334 made . . . cuckold** i.e., gave Lucifer his horns,
the sign of cuckoldry   **334–335 and swore . . . liegeman** and made the
devil take an oath of allegiance as a true subject   **335 Welsh hook**
curved-bladed pike lacking the cross shape of the sword on which such
oaths were usually sworn

POINS   Owen Glendower.

FALSTAFF   Owen, Owen, the same; and his son-in-law Mortimer, and old Northumberland, and that sprightly Scot of Scots, Douglas, that runs a-horseback up a hill perpendicular—

PRINCE   He that rides at high speed, and with his pistol kills a sparrow flying.

FALSTAFF   You have hit it.   344

PRINCE   So did he never the sparrow.

FALSTAFF   Well, that rascal hath good mettle in him; he will not run.

PRINCE   Why, what a rascal art thou then to praise him so for running!

FALSTAFF   A-horseback, ye cuckoo; but afoot he will not budge a foot.

PRINCE   Yes, Jack, upon instinct.

FALSTAFF   I grant ye, upon instinct. Well, he is there too, and one Mordake, and a thousand blue-caps more.   354 Worcester is stolen away tonight. Thy father's beard is turned white with the news. You may buy land now as cheap as stinking mackerel.

PRINCE   Why, then, it is like, if there come a hot June   358 and this civil buffeting hold, we shall buy maiden-   359 heads as they buy hobnails, by the hundreds.

FALSTAFF   By the Mass, lad, thou sayest true; it is like we shall have good trading that way. But tell me, Hal, art not thou horrible afeard? Thou being heir apparent, could the world pick thee out three such enemies again as that fiend Douglas, that spirit Percy, and that devil Glendower? Art thou not horribly afraid? Doth not thy blood thrill at it?

PRINCE   Not a whit, i' faith. I lack some of thy instinct.

FALSTAFF   Well, thou wilt be horribly chid tomorrow   369 when thou comest to thy father. If thou love me, prac-tice an answer.

PRINCE   Do thou stand for my father and examine me upon the particulars of my life.

FALSTAFF   Shall I? Content. This chair shall be my state,   374

344 hit it described it exactly (though the Prince takes *hit* literally in l. 345)   **354 blue-caps** Scottish soldiers   **358 like** likely   **359 hold** continues   **369 chid** chided   **374 state** chair of state, throne

this dagger my scepter, and this cushion my crown.

[*Falstaff establishes himself on his "throne."*]

PRINCE   Thy state is taken for a joint stool, thy golden 376
scepter for a leaden dagger, and thy precious rich 377
crown for a pitiful bald crown!

FALSTAFF   Well, an the fire of grace be not quite out of 379
thee, now shalt thou be moved. Give me a cup of sack
to make my eyes look red, that it may be thought I
have wept; for I must speak in passion, and I will do
it in King Cambyses' vein. 383

PRINCE   Well, here is my leg.   [*He bows.*]

FALSTAFF   And here is my speech. Stand aside, nobility.

HOSTESS   O Jesu, this is excellent sport, i' faith!

FALSTAFF

Weep not, sweet queen, for trickling tears are vain.

HOSTESS   O, the Father, how he holds his countenance! 389

FALSTAFF

For God's sake, lords, convey my tristful queen, 390
For tears do stop the floodgates of her eyes. 391

HOSTESS   O Jesu, he doth it as like one of these harlotry 392
players as ever I see! 393

FALSTAFF

Peace, good pint pot; peace, good tickle-brain.— 394
Harry, I do not only marvel where thou spendest thy
time, but also how thou art accompanied; for though
the camomile, the more it is trodden on the faster it 397
grows, yet youth, the more it is wasted the sooner it 398
wears. That thou art my son I have partly thy mother's 399
word, partly my own opinion, but chiefly a villainous

---

376 joint stool a stool made by a joiner or furniture maker. (To "take
someone for a joint stool" is to offer an intentionally silly apology for
overlooking that person, as in *King Lear*, 3.6.52. Hal suggests that
Falstaff's *state* is ridiculous [punning on *state*, throne].)   **377 leaden** of
soft metal, hence inferior   **379 an** if   **383 in . . . vein** i.e., in the ranting
and (by Shakespeare's time) old-fashioned style of Thomas Preston's
Cambyses, an early Elizabethan tragedy   **389 the Father** i.e., in God's
name.   **holds his countenance** keeps a straight face   **390 convey** escort
away.   **tristful** sorrowing   **391 stop** fill   **392 harlotry** scurvy, vaga-
bond   **393 players** actors   **394 tickle-brain** (A slang term for strong
liquor, here applied as a nickname for the tavern hostess.)
397–399 camomile . . . wears (This parodies the style of Lyly's *Euphues*
and exaggerates the balance and alliteration of the style.)   **camomile** an
aromatic creeping herb whose flowers and leaves are used medicinally

trick of thine eye and a foolish hanging of thy nether 401
lip that doth warrant me. If then thou be son to me, 402
here lies the point: why, being son to me, art thou so
pointed at? Shall the blessed sun of heaven prove a
micher and eat blackberries? A question not to be 405
asked. Shall the son of England prove a thief and take
purses? A question to be asked. There is a thing,
Harry, which thou hast often heard of, and it is known
to many in our land by the name of pitch. This pitch, 409
as ancient writers do report, doth defile; so doth the 410
company thou keepest. For, Harry, now I do not speak
to thee in drink but in tears, not in pleasure but in
passion, not in words only but in woes also. And yet
there is a virtuous man whom I have often noted in
thy company, but I know not his name.

PRINCE   What manner of man, an it like Your Majesty? 416

FALSTAFF   A goodly portly man, i' faith, and a corpulent; 417
of a cheerful look, a pleasing eye, and a most noble
carriage; and, as I think, his age some fifty, or, by 'r
Lady, inclining to threescore; and now I remember me,
his name is Falstaff. If that man should be lewdly 421
given, he deceiveth me; for, Harry, I see virtue in his
looks. If then the tree may be known by the fruit, as 423
the fruit by the tree, then peremptorily I speak it, 424
there is virtue in that Falstaff. Him keep with, the rest
banish. And tell me now, thou naughty varlet, tell me,
where hast thou been this month?

PRINCE   Dost thou speak like a king? Do thou stand for
me, and I'll play my father.

FALSTAFF   Depose me? If thou dost it half so gravely, so
majestically, both in word and matter, hang me up by
the heels for a rabbit-sucker or a poulter's hare.   432

        [*Hal takes Falstaff's place on the "throne."*]

PRINCE   Well, here I am set.   433

FALSTAFF   And here I stand. Judge, my masters.

---

401 trick trait   **402 warrant** assure   **405 micher** truant   **409–410 This
. . . defile** (An allusion to the familiar proverb from Ecclesiasticus 13:1
about the defilement of touching pitch.)   **pitch** a sticky, black residue
from the distillation of tar, used to seal wood from moisture   **416 an it
like** if it please   **417 portly** (1) stately (2) corpulent   **421 lewdly** wick-
edly   **423 If . . . by the fruit** (See Matthew 12:33.)   **424 peremptorily**
decisively   **432 rabbit-sucker** unweaned rabbit.   **poulter's** poulterer's
433 set seated

PRINCE   Now, Harry, whence come you?

FALSTAFF   My noble lord, from Eastcheap.

PRINCE   The complaints I hear of thee are grievous.

FALSTAFF   'Sblood, my lord, they are false.—Nay, I'll 438
tickle ye for a young prince, i' faith. 439

PRINCE   Swearest thou, ungracious boy? Henceforth
ne'er look on me. Thou art violently carried away from
grace. There is a devil haunts thee in the likeness of an
old fat man; a tun of man is thy companion. Why dost 443
thou converse with that trunk of humors, that bolting- 444
hutch of beastliness, that swollen parcel of dropsies, 445
that huge bombard of sack, that stuffed cloak-bag of 446
guts, that roasted Manningtree ox with the pudding in 447
his belly, that reverend Vice, that gray Iniquity, that 448
father ruffian, that vanity in years? Wherein is he 449
good but to taste sack and drink it? Wherein neat and
cleanly but to carve a capon and eat it? Wherein cun- 451
ning but in craft? Wherein crafty but in villainy? 452
Wherein villainous but in all things? Wherein worthy but in nothing?

FALSTAFF   I would Your Grace would take me with you. 455
Whom means Your Grace?

PRINCE   That villainous abominable misleader of youth,
Falstaff, that old white-bearded Satan.

FALSTAFF   My lord, the man I know.

PRINCE   I know thou dost.

FALSTAFF   But to say I know more harm in him than in
myself were to say more than I know. That he is old,
the more the pity, his white hairs do witness it; but
that he is, saving your reverence, a whoremaster, that 464
I utterly deny. If sack and sugar be a fault, God help
the wicked! If to be old and merry be a sin, then many

---

438 'Sblood i.e., by Christ's blood   **439 tickle ye for** amuse you in the
role of   **443 tun** (1) large barrel (2) ton   **444 converse** associate.
humors body fluids, diseases   **444–445 bolting-hutch** large bin
446 bombard leathern drinking vessel   **447 Manningtree ox** (Manningtree, a town in Essex, had noted fairs where, no doubt, oxen were
roasted whole.)   **pudding** sausage   **448 Vice, Iniquity** (Allegorical
names for the chief comic character and tempter in morality plays.)
449 vanity person given to worldly desires   **451 cleanly** deft
451–452 cunning skillful   **455 take me with you** i.e., let me catch up
with your meaning   **464 saving your reverence** i.e., with my apology for
using offensive language

an old host that I know is damned. If to be fat be to be 467
hated, then Pharaoh's lean kine are to be loved. No, 468
my good lord, banish Peto, banish Bardolph, banish
Poins; but for sweet Jack Falstaff, kind Jack Falstaff,
true Jack Falstaff, valiant Jack Falstaff, and therefore
more valiant being as he is old Jack Falstaff, banish
not him thy Harry's company, banish not him thy
Harry's company—banish plump Jack, and banish all
the world.

PRINCE   I do, I will.   [*A knocking.*
                Exeunt Hostess, Francis, and Bardolph.]

    Enter Bardolph, running.

BARDOLPH   O, my lord, my lord! The sheriff with a most
monstrous watch is at the door.   478

FALSTAFF   Out, ye rogue! Play out the play. I have much
to say in the behalf of that Falstaff.

    Enter the Hostess.

HOSTESS   O Jesu, my lord, my lord!

PRINCE   Heigh, heigh! The devil rides upon a fiddle- 482
stick. What's the matter?   483

HOSTESS   The sheriff and all the watch are at the door.
They are come to search the house. Shall I let them in?

FALSTAFF   Dost thou hear, Hal? Never call a true piece of 486
gold a counterfeit. Thou art essentially made without 487
seeming so.   488

PRINCE   And thou a natural coward without instinct.

FALSTAFF   I deny your major. If you will deny the sher- 490
iff, so; if not, let him enter. If I become not a cart as 491
well as another man, a plague on my bringing up! I 492
hope I shall as soon be strangled with a halter as another.

---

467 host innkeeper   **468 Pharaoh's lean kine** (See Genesis 41:3–4,
18–21.)   **478 watch** posse of constables   **482–483 The . . . fiddlestick**
i.e., here's much ado about nothing   **486–488 Dost . . . seeming so** (In
this difficult passage, Falstaff seems to suggest that he is true gold, not
counterfeit, and so should not be betrayed to the watch by the Prince,
who, he hopes, is not merely playacting at the tavern but is truly one of
its madcap members.)   **490 deny your major** reject your major prem-
ise. **deny the** refuse entrance to the   **491 become** befit, adorn. **cart**
i.e., hangman's cart   **492 bringing up** (1) upbringing (2) being brought
before the authorities to be hanged

PRINCE Go hide thee behind the arras. The rest walk 495
up above. Now, my masters, for a true face and good 496
conscience.

FALSTAFF Both which I have had, but their date is out, 498
and therefore I'll hide me.

                    [*He hides behind the arras.*]

PRINCE Call in the sheriff.

               [*Exeunt all except the Prince and Peto.*]

    Enter Sheriff and the Carrier.

Now, Master Sheriff, what is your will with me?

SHERIFF
First, pardon me, my lord. A hue and cry
Hath followed certain men unto this house.

PRINCE What men?

SHERIFF
One of them is well known, my gracious lord,
A gross fat man.

CARRIER   As fat as butter.

PRINCE
The man, I do assure you, is not here,
For I myself at this time have employed him.
And, Sheriff, I will engage my word to thee   509
That I will, by tomorrow dinnertime,   510
Send him to answer thee, or any man,
For anything he shall be charged withal;
And so let me entreat you leave the house.

SHERIFF
I will, my lord. There are two gentlemen
Have in this robbery lost three hundred marks.

PRINCE
It may be so. If he have robbed these men,
He shall be answerable; and so farewell.

SHERIFF Good night, my noble lord.

PRINCE
I think it is good morrow, is it not?   519

SHERIFF
Indeed, my lord, I think it be two o'clock.

                    Exit [*with Carrier*].

495 arras wall hanging of tapestry **496 up above** upstairs **498 date is
out** time is past **509 engage** pledge **510 dinnertime** i.e., about noon
519 morrow morning

PRINCE This oily rascal is known as well as Paul's. Go 521
   call him forth.
PETO [*Discovering Falstaff*] Falstaff!—Fast asleep be-
   hind the arras, and snorting like a horse.
PRINCE Hark, how hard he fetches breath. Search his
   pockets. (*He searcheth his pockets, and findeth certain
   papers.*) What hast thou found?
PETO Nothing but papers, my lord.
PRINCE Let's see what they be. Read them.
PETO [*Reads*]
        Item, A capon, ...2s. 2d.
        Item, Sauce, ... 4d.
        Item, Sack, two gallons, ...5s. 8d.
        Item, Anchovies and sack after supper. . .2s. 6d.
        Item, Bread, ... ob.   534
PRINCE O, monstrous! But one halfpennyworth of
   bread to this intolerable deal of sack? What there is
   else, keep close; we'll read it at more advantage. There 537
   let him sleep till day. I'll to the court in the morning.
   We must all to the wars, and thy place shall be honorable. I'll procure this fat rogue a charge of foot, and 540
   I know his death will be a march of twelve score. The 541
   money shall be paid back again with advantage. Be 542
   with me betimes in the morning; and so, good mor- 543
   row, Peto.
PETO Good morrow, good my lord.   545
              *Exeunt [separately. Falstaff is concealed
                      once more behind the arras*].

                           ❖

521 Paul's Saint Paul's Cathedral   **534 ob.** obolus, i.e., halfpenny
537 close hidden.   **advantage** favorable opportunity   **540 charge of foot**
command of a company of infantry   **541 twelve score** i.e., 240 yards
542 advantage interest   **543 betimes** early   **545 s.d. Exeunt . . . arras**
(Onstage, the arras is evidently arranged so that Falstaff can exit behind
it once the scene is over.)

3.1   *Enter Hotspur, Worcester, Lord Mortimer, [and]
Owen Glendower.*

MORTIMER
  These promises are fair, the parties sure,
  And our induction full of prosperous hope.   2
HOTSPUR
  Lord Mortimer, and cousin Glendower,
  Will you sit down? And uncle Worcester—

                                        [*They sit.*]

  A plague upon it, I have forgot the map.
GLENDOWER [*Producing a map*]
  No, here it is. Sit, cousin Percy,
  Sit, good cousin Hotspur—for by that name
  As oft as Lancaster doth speak of you   8
  His cheek looks pale, and with a rising sigh
  He wisheth you in heaven.
HOTSPUR   And you in hell,
  As oft as he hears Owen Glendower spoke of.
GLENDOWER
  I cannot blame him. At my nativity
  The front of heaven was full of fiery shapes,   13
  Of burning cressets, and at my birth   14
  The frame and huge foundation of the earth
  Shaked like a coward.
HOTSPUR   Why, so it would have done
  At the same season if your mother's cat
  Had but kittened, though yourself had never been born.
GLENDOWER
  I say the earth did shake when I was born.
HOTSPUR
  And I say the earth was not of my mind,
  If you suppose as fearing you it shook.

3.1. Location: Wales. Glendower's residence. (Holinshed places a meeting of the rebel deputies at Bangor in the Archdeacon's house, but in
this present "unhistorical" scene as invented by Shakespeare, Glendower is host throughout.) Seats are provided onstage.
2 induction beginning.   prosperous hope hope of prospering
8 Lancaster i.e., King Henry, here demoted to Duke of Lancaster
13 front brow, face (as also at l. 36)   14 cressets lights burning in
baskets atop long poles; hence, meteors

GLENDOWER
  The heavens were all on fire; the earth did tremble.
HOTSPUR
  O, then the earth shook to see the heavens on fire,
  And not in fear of your nativity.
  Diseasèd nature oftentimes breaks forth
  In strange eruptions; oft the teeming earth
  Is with a kind of colic pinched and vexed
  By the imprisoning of unruly wind
  Within her womb, which, for enlargement striving,   29
  Shakes the old beldam earth and topples down   30
  Steeples and moss-grown towers. At your birth
  Our grandam earth, having this distemp'rature,
  In passion shook.
GLENDOWER   Cousin, of many men   33
  I do not bear these crossings. Give me leave   34
  To tell you once again that at my birth
  The front of heaven was full of fiery shapes,
  The goats ran from the mountains, and the herds
  Were strangely clamorous to the frighted fields.   38
  These signs have marked me extraordinary,
  And all the courses of my life do show
  I am not in the roll of common men.
  Where is he living, clipped in with the sea   42
  That chides the banks of England, Scotland, Wales,
  Which calls me pupil, or hath read to me?   44
  And bring him out that is but woman's son   45
  Can trace me in the tedious ways of art   46
  And hold me pace in deep experiments.   47
HOTSPUR
  I think there's no man speaks better Welsh.   48
  I'll to dinner.
MORTIMER
  Peace, cousin Percy; you will make him mad.

---

29 enlargement release   **30 beldam** grandmother   **33 passion** suffering.   **of** from   **34 crossings** contradictions   **38 clamorous** noisy   **42 he**
anyone.   **clipped in with** enclosed by   **44 Which** who.   **read to** in-
structed   **45 bring him out** produce any man   **46 Can . . . art** who can
follow me in the laborious ways of magic   **47 hold me pace** keep up
with me.   **deep** occult   **48 speaks better Welsh** (Hotspur hides an insult
behind the literal meaning, since "to speak Welsh" meant colloquially
both "to boast" and "to speak nonsense.")

GLENDOWER
  I can call spirits from the vasty deep.   51
HOTSPUR
  Why, so can I, or so can any man;
  But will they come when you do call for them?
GLENDOWER
  Why, I can teach you, cousin, to command the devil.
HOTSPUR
  And I can teach thee, coz, to shame the devil
  By telling truth. Tell truth and shame the devil.
  If thou have power to raise him, bring him hither,
  And I'll be sworn I have power to shame him hence.
  O, while you live, tell truth and shame the devil!
MORTIMER
  Come, come, no more of this unprofitable chat.
GLENDOWER
  Three times hath Henry Bolingbroke made head   61
  Against my power; thrice from the banks of Wye   62
  And sandy-bottomed Severn have I sent him
  Bootless home and weather-beaten back.   64
HOTSPUR
  Home without boots, and in foul weather too!
  How scapes he agues, in the devil's name?   66
GLENDOWER
  Come, here is the map. Shall we divide our right
  According to our threefold order ta'en?   68
MORTIMER
  The Archdeacon hath divided it   69
  Into three limits very equally: 70
  England, from Trent and Severn hitherto,   71
  By south and east is to my part assigned;
  All westward, Wales beyond the Severn shore,
  And all the fertile land within that bound,
  To Owen Glendower; and, dear coz, to you
  The remnant northward, lying off from Trent.

51 call summon. (But Hotspur sardonically replies in the sense of "call
out to," whether or not there is any response.) **vasty deep** lower
world **61 made head** raised a force **62 power** army **64 Bootless**
without advantage (but Hotspur quibbles on the sense of "barefoot")
66 agues fevers **68 order ta'en** arrangements made **69 Archdeacon**
i.e., the Archdeacon of Bangor, in whose house, according to Holinshed,
a meeting took place between deputies of the rebel leaders **70 limits**
regions **71 hitherto** to this point

And our indentures tripartite are drawn,   77
Which being sealèd interchangeably—
A business that this night may execute—   79
Tomorrow, cousin Percy, you and I
And my good lord of Worcester will set forth
To meet your father and the Scottish power,
As is appointed us, at Shrewsbury.
My father Glendower is not ready yet,   84
Nor shall we need his help these fourteen days.
[*To Glendower*.] Within that space you may have
   drawn together   86
Your tenants, friends, and neighboring gentlemen.

GLENDOWER
A shorter time shall send me to you, lords;
And in my conduct shall your ladies come,   89
From whom you now must steal and take no leave,
For there will be a world of water shed
Upon the parting of your wives and you.

HOTSPUR [*Consulting the map*]
Methinks my moiety, north from Burton here,   93
In quantity equals not one of yours.
See how this river comes me cranking in   95
And cuts me from the best of all my land
A huge half-moon, a monstrous cantle out.   97
I'll have the current in this place dammed up,
And here the smug and silver Trent shall run   99
In a new channel, fair and evenly.
It shall not wind with such a deep indent
To rob me of so rich a bottom here.   102

GLENDOWER
Not wind? It shall, it must! You see it doth.

MORTIMER
Yea, but mark how he bears his course and runs me up 104
With like advantage on the other side,

77 tripartite i.e., drawn up in triplicate, each document sealed *interchangeably* (l. 78) with the seal of all signatories. **drawn** drawn up
79 this night may execute may be carried out tonight **84 father** i.e.,
father-in-law **86 may** will be able to **89 conduct** escort **93 moiety**
share **95 comes me cranking in** comes bending in on my share. (The
Trent, by turning northward instead of continuing eastward into the
Wash, cuts Hotspur off from rich land in Lincolnshire and vicinity.)
97 cantle piece **99 smug** smooth **102 bottom** valley **104 runs me**
runs. (*Me* is used colloquially.)

Gelding the opposèd continent as much   106
As on the other side it takes from you.

WORCESTER
Yea, but a little charge will trench him here   108
And on this north side win this cape of land;
And then he runs straight and even.

HOTSPUR
I'll have it so. A little charge will do it.

GLENDOWER   I'll not have it altered.

HOTSPUR   Will not you?

GLENDOWER   No, nor you shall not.

HOTSPUR   Who shall say me nay?

GLENDOWER   Why, that will I.

HOTSPUR
Let me not understand you, then; speak it in Welsh.

GLENDOWER
I can speak English, lord, as well as you;
For I was trained up in the English court,
Where, being but young, I framèd to the harp   120
Many an English ditty lovely well,
And gave the tongue a helpful ornament—   122
A virtue that was never seen in you.

HOTSPUR
Marry, and I am glad of it with all my heart!
I had rather be a kitten and cry "mew"
Than one of these same meter balladmongers.
I had rather hear a brazen can'stick turned   127
Or a dry wheel grate on the axletree,   128
And that would set my teeth nothing on edge,   129
Nothing so much as mincing poetry.
'Tis like the forced gait of a shuffling nag.   131

GLENDOWER   Come, you shall have Trent turned.

HOTSPUR
I do not care. I'll give thrice so much land

106 Gelding . . . continent cutting off from the land which it bounds on
the opposite side. (The Trent's southerly loop from Stoke to Burton
deprives Mortimer of a piece of land, just as its later northerly course
deprives Hotspur.)   **108 charge** expenditure.   **trench** provide a new
channel   **120 framèd to the harp** set to harp accompaniment   **122 gave
. . . ornament** i.e., added to the words a pleasing ornament of music;
also, gave to the English tongue the ornament of music and poetry
127 can'stick turned candlestick turned on a lathe   **128 axletree** axle
129 nothing not at all   **131 shuffling** hobbled

To any well-deserving friend;
But in the way of bargain, mark ye me,
I'll cavil on the ninth part of a hair.   136
Are the indentures drawn? Shall we be gone?   137

GLENDOWER
The moon shines fair; you may away by night.
I'll haste the writer and withal   139
Break with your wives of your departure hence.   140
I am afraid my daughter will run mad,
So much she doteth on her Mortimer.   *Exit.*

MORTIMER
Fie, cousin Percy, how you cross my father!

HOTSPUR
I cannot choose. Sometimes he angers me
With telling me of the moldwarp and the ant,   145
Of the dreamer Merlin and his prophecies,   146
And of a dragon and a finless fish,
A clip-winged griffin and a moulten raven,   148
A couching lion and a ramping cat,   149
And such a deal of skimble-skamble stuff   150
As puts me from my faith. I tell you what: 151
He held me last night at least nine hours
In reckoning up the several devils' names   153
That were his lackeys. I cried "Hum," and "Well, go to,"
But marked him not a word. O, he is as tedious
As a tirèd horse, a railing wife,
Worse than a smoky house. I had rather live
With cheese and garlic in a windmill, far,
Than feed on cates and have him talk to me   159
In any summer house in Christendom.

---

136 cavil . . . hair i.e., argue about the most trivial detail   **137 drawn**
drawn up   **139 haste** hurry.   **writer** i.e., scrivener who would be drawing the indentures.   **withal** also   **140 Break with** inform   **145 moldwarp** mole. (Holinshed tells us that the division was arranged because
of a prophecy that represented King Henry as the mole and the others
as the dragon, the lion, and the wolf, who should divide the land among
them.)   **146 Merlin** the bard, prophet, and magician of Arthurian story,
Welsh in origin   **148 griffin** a fabulous beast, half lion, half eagle.
moulten having molted   **149 couching** couchant, crouching. (Heraldic
term.)   **ramping** rampant, advancing on its hind legs. (Hotspur is
ridiculing the heraldic emblems that Glendower holds so dear.)
150 skimble-skamble foolish, nonsensical   **151 puts . . . faith** drives me
from my (Christian) faith   **153 several** various   **159 cates** delicacies

MORTIMER
    In faith, he is a worthy gentleman,
    Exceedingly well read, and profited   162
    In strange concealments, valiant as a lion   163
    And wondrous affable, and as bountiful
    As mines of India. Shall I tell you, cousin?
    He holds your temper in a high respect   166
    And curbs himself even of his natural scope   167
    When you come 'cross his humor. Faith, he does.   168
    I warrant you that man is not alive
    Might so have tempted him as you have done   170
    Without the taste of danger and reproof.
    But do not use it oft, let me entreat you.

WORCESTER
    In faith, my lord, you are too willful-blame,   173
    And since your coming hither have done enough
    To put him quite beside his patience.   175
    You must needs learn, lord, to amend this fault.
    Though sometimes it show greatness, courage, blood—   177
    And that's the dearest grace it renders you—   178
    Yet oftentimes it doth present harsh rage,   179
    Defect of manners, want of government,   180
    Pride, haughtiness, opinion, and disdain,   181
    The least of which haunting a nobleman
    Loseth men's hearts and leaves behind a stain
    Upon the beauty of all parts besides,   184
    Beguiling them of commendation.   185

HOTSPUR
    Well, I am schooled. Good manners be your speed!   186
    Here comes our wives, and let us take our leave.

    Enter Glendower with the ladies.

MORTIMER
    This is the deadly spite that angers me: 188
    My wife can speak no English, I no Welsh.

162 profited proficient   **163 concealments** occult practices   **166 temper**
temperament   **167 scope** freedom of speech   **168 come 'cross** contradict   **170 Might** who could   **173 willful-blame** blameworthy for too
much self-will   **175 beside** out of   **177 blood** spirit   **178 dearest grace**
best credit   **179 present** represent   **180 want of government** lack of
self-control   **181 opinion** vanity, arrogance   **184 all parts besides** all
other abilities   **185 Beguiling** depriving   **186 be your speed** give you
good fortune   **188 spite** vexation

GLENDOWER
   My daughter weeps. She'll not part with you;
   She'll be a soldier too, she'll to the wars.

MORTIMER
   Good Father, tell her that she and my aunt Percy   192
   Shall follow in your conduct speedily.
                    Glendower speaks to her in Welsh,
                    and she answers him in the same.

GLENDOWER
   She is desperate here; a peevish self-willed harlotry,   194
   One that no persuasion can do good upon.
                         The lady speaks in Welsh.

MORTIMER
   I understand thy looks. That pretty Welsh   196
   Which thou pourest down from these swelling heavens   197
   I am too perfect in; and, but for shame,   198
   In such a parley should I answer thee.   199
                         The lady again in Welsh.
   I understand thy kisses and thou mine,
   And that's a feeling disputation.   201
   But I will never be a truant, love,
   Till I have learned thy language; for thy tongue
   Makes Welsh as sweet as ditties highly penned,   204
   Sung by a fair queen in a summer's bower,
   With ravishing division, to her lute.   206

GLENDOWER
   Nay, if you melt, then will she run mad.   207
                    The lady speaks again in Welsh.

MORTIMER
   O, I am ignorance itself in this!

GLENDOWER
   She bids you on the wanton rushes lay you down   209
   And rest your gentle head upon her lap,

---

192 aunt (Percy's wife, here called Kate, was aunt of Edmund Mortimer, the fifth Earl of March, but was sister-in-law to the Sir Edward Mortimer who married Glendower's daughter.)   **194 desperate here**
adamant on this point (i.e., her decision to accompany Mortimer).
peevish self-willed harlotry childish, willful, silly wench   **196 That
pretty Welsh** i.e., your eloquent tears   **197 heavens** i.e., eyes
198 perfect proficient   **199 such a parley** i.e., the same language (of
weeping)   **201 disputation** conversation, debate   **204 highly** eloquently,
nobly   **206 division** variation (in music)   **207 melt** i.e., weep
209 wanton soft, luxurious.   **rushes** (Used as floor covering.)

And she will sing the song that pleaseth you
And on your eyelids crown the god of sleep,   212
Charming your blood with pleasing heaviness,   213
Making such difference twixt wake and sleep
As is the difference betwixt day and night
The hour before the heavenly-harnessed team   216
Begins his golden progress in the east.

MORTIMER
With all my heart I'll sit and hear her sing.
By that time will our book, I think, be drawn.   219

GLENDOWER   Do so;
And those musicians that shall play to you
Hang in the air a thousand leagues from hence,
And straight they shall be here. Sit, and attend.
                    [*Mortimer reclines with his head*
                        in his wife's lap.]

HOTSPUR   Come, Kate, thou art perfect in lying down;
come, quick, quick, that I may lay my head in thy lap.

LADY PERCY   Go, ye giddy goose.
                    [*Hotspur lies with his head*
                        in Kate's lap.] *The music plays.*

HOTSPUR
Now I perceive the devil understands Welsh;
And 'tis no marvel he is so humorous.   228
By 'r Lady, he is a good musician.

LADY PERCY   Then should you be nothing but musical,
for you are altogether governed by humors. Lie still, ye
thief, and hear the lady sing in Welsh.

HOTSPUR   I had rather hear Lady, my brach, howl in   233
Irish.

LADY PERCY   Wouldst thou have thy head broken?   235

HOTSPUR   No.

LADY PERCY   Then be still.

HOTSPUR   Neither, 'tis a woman's fault.   238

LADY PERCY   Now God help thee!

HOTSPUR   To the Welsh lady's bed.

LADY PERCY   What's that?

---

212 **crown** give sway to   213 **heaviness** drowsiness   216 **the heavenly-
harnessed team** i.e., the team of horses drawing the chariot of the sun
219 **book** document, indentures   228 **humorous** whimsical, capri-
cious   233 **brach** bitch hound   235 **broken** i.e., struck so as to break
the skin   238 **Neither** i.e., I won't do that either

HOTSPUR   Peace, she sings.

Here the lady sings a Welsh song.

Come, Kate, I'll have your song too.

LADY PERCY   Not mine, in good sooth.

HOTSPUR   Not yours, in good sooth! Heart, you swear 245
like a comfit maker's wife. "Not you, in good sooth," 246
and "as true as I live," and "as God shall mend me,"
and "as sure as day,"
And givest such sarcenet surety for thy oaths 249
As if thou never walk'st further than Finsbury. 250
Swear me, Kate, like a lady as thou art,
A good mouth-filling oath, and leave "in sooth,"
And such protest of pepper-gingerbread, 253
To velvet-guards and Sunday citizens. 254
Come, sing.

LADY PERCY   I will not sing.

HOTSPUR   'Tis the next way to turn tailor, or be redbreast 257
teacher. An the indentures be drawn, I'll away within 258
these two hours; and so, come in when ye will.   *Exit.*

GLENDOWER

Come, come, Lord Mortimer. You are as slow
As hot Lord Percy is on fire to go.
By this our book is drawn; we'll but seal, 262
And then to horse immediately.

MORTIMER   With all my heart.   *Exeunt.*

❖

3.2   *Enter the King, Prince of Wales, and others.*

KING

Lords, give us leave. The Prince of Wales and I
Must have some private conference; but be near at hand,

---

245 Heart i.e., by Christ's heart   **246 comfit maker's** confectioner's
249 sarcenet soft, flimsy (from the soft silken material known as *sarce-net*)   **250 Finsbury** a field just outside London frequented by the London citizenry. (Hotspur jokes with Kate as though she were a citizen's wife, using the pious and modest oaths of such people.)   **253 protest . . . gingerbread** i.e., mealy-mouthed protestations   **254 velvet-guards** i.e., wives who wear velvet trimming   **257 next** nearest, quickest.   **turn tailor** (Tailors were noted for singing and effeminacy.)   **257–258 be redbreast teacher** i.e., teach birds to sing. (Hotspur is expressing his contempt for music.)   **262 By this** by this time.   **but** just

3.2. Location: London. The royal court.

For we shall presently have need of you.

Exeunt Lords.

I know not whether God will have it so
For some displeasing service I have done,
That in his secret doom out of my blood   6
He'll breed revengement and a scourge for me;
But thou dost in thy passages of life   8
Make me believe that thou art only marked   9
For the hot vengeance and the rod of heaven   10
To punish my mistreadings. Tell me else,   11
Could such inordinate and low desires,   12
Such poor, such bare, such lewd, such mean attempts,   13
Such barren pleasures, rude society,
As thou art matched withal and grafted to,   15
Accompany the greatness of thy blood
And hold their level with thy princely heart?   17

PRINCE
So please Your Majesty, I would I could
Quit all offenses with as clear excuse   19
As well as I am doubtless I can purge   20
Myself of many I am charged withal.
Yet such extenuation let me beg
As, in reproof of many tales devised,   23
Which oft the ear of greatness needs must hear
By smiling pickthanks and base newsmongers,   25
I may, for some things true, wherein my youth
Hath faulty wandered and irregular,
Find pardon on my true submission.   28

KING
God pardon thee! Yet let me wonder, Harry,
At thy affections, which do hold a wing   30
Quite from the flight of all thy ancestors.   31

---

6 **doom** judgment. **blood** offspring   8 **passages** course, conduct
9–11 **thou . . . mistreadings** (1) you are marked as the means of heaven's
vengeance against me, or (2) you are marked to suffer heaven's vengeance because of my sins   11 **else** how otherwise   12 **inordinate** (1) im-
moderate (2) unworthy of your rank   13 **lewd** low, base. **attempts**
undertakings   15 **withal** with   17 **hold their level** claim equality
19 **Quit** acquit myself of   20 **doubtless** certain   23 **in reproof** upon
disproof   25 **By** from. **pickthanks** flatterers. **newsmongers** talebearers   28 **submission** admission of fault   30 **affections** inclinations.
hold a wing fly a course   31 **from** at variance with

Thy place in Council thou hast rudely lost,   32
Which by thy younger brother is supplied,
And art almost an alien to the hearts
Of all the court and princes of my blood.
The hope and expectation of thy time   36
Is ruined, and the soul of every man
Prophetically do forethink thy fall.
Had I so lavish of my presence been,
So common-hackneyed in the eyes of men,   40
So stale and cheap to vulgar company,
Opinion, that did help me to the crown,   42
Had still kept loyal to possession   43
And left me in reputeless banishment,
A fellow of no mark nor likelihood.   45
By being seldom seen, I could not stir
But like a comet I was wondered at,
That men would tell their children, "This is he!"
Others would say, "Where, which is Bolingbroke?"
And then I stole all courtesy from heaven,   50
And dressed myself in such humility
That I did pluck allegiance from men's hearts,
Loud shouts and salutations from their mouths,
Even in the presence of the crownèd King.
Thus did I keep my person fresh and new,
My presence, like a robe pontifical,   56
Ne'er seen but wondered at; and so my state,   57
Seldom but sumptuous, showed like a feast   58
And won by rareness such solemnity.   59
The skipping King, he ambled up and down   60
With shallow jesters and rash bavin wits,   61
Soon kindled and soon burnt; carded his state,   62

32 **rudely** by violence. (According to an apocryphal story, Hal boxed the
ears of the Lord Chief Justice and was sent to prison for it; see *2 Henry
IV,* 1.2.54–55, 192, and 5.2.70–71.)   36 **time** time of life, youth
40 **common-hackneyed** cheapened, vulgarized   42 **Opinion** i.e., public
opinion   43 **to possession** i.e., to Richard II's sovereignty   45 **mark**
importance.   **likelihood** likelihood of success   50 **I . . . heaven** i.e., I
assumed a bearing of the utmost graciousness   56 **pontifical** like that
of a pope or archbishop   57 **state** magnificence in public appear-
ances   58 **Seldom** infrequent   59 **such solemnity** i.e., the solemnity
appropriate to a festival   60 **skipping** flighty   61 **bavin** brushwood,
soon burnt out   62 **carded** debased. (A term applied to the adulteration
or combing of wool.)   **state** royal status

Mingled his royalty with capering fools,
Had his great name profanèd with their scorns,   64
And gave his countenance, against his name,   65
To laugh at gibing boys and stand the push   66
Of every beardless vain comparative;   67
Grew a companion to the common streets,
Enfeoffed himself to popularity,   69
That, being daily swallowed by men's eyes,
They surfeited with honey and began
To loathe the taste of sweetness, whereof a little
More than a little is by much too much.
So when he had occasion to be seen,
He was but as the cuckoo is in June,
Heard, not regarded—seen, but with such eyes
As, sick and blunted with community,   77
Afford no extraordinary gaze,
Such as is bent on sunlike majesty
When it shines seldom in admiring eyes;
But rather drowsed and hung their eyelids down,
Slept in his face, and rendered such aspect   82
As cloudy men use to their adversaries,   83
Being with his presence glutted, gorged, and full.
And in that very line, Harry, standest thou;
For thou hast lost thy princely privilege
With vile participation. Not an eye   87
But is aweary of thy common sight,
Save mine, which hath desired to see thee more—
Which now doth that I would not have it do,   90
Make blind itself with foolish tenderness.   91

PRINCE
I shall hereafter, my thrice gracious lord,
Be more myself.

KING   For all the world

64 their scorns i.e., the scornful opinion people had of these favorites
65 gave . . . name lent his authority, to the detriment of his royal dignity
and reputation   **66 stand the push** put up with the impudence
67 comparative maker of comparisons, wisecracker   **69 Enfeoffed
himself** gave himself up   **77 community** commonness   **82 in his face**
right before his eyes.   **aspect** look   **83 cloudy** sullen. (Also refers to the
image of the sun.)   **87 vile participation** base association or companion-
ship   **90 that** that which   **91 tenderness** i.e., tears

As thou art to this hour was Richard then
When I from France set foot at Ravenspurgh,
And even as I was then is Percy now.
Now, by my scepter, and my soul to boot,   97
He hath more worthy interest to the state   98
Than thou the shadow of succession.   99
For of no right, nor color like to right,   100
He doth fill fields with harness in the realm,   101
Turns head against the lion's armèd jaws,   102
And, being no more in debt to years than thou,   103
Leads ancient lords and reverend bishops on
To bloody battles and to bruising arms.
What never-dying honor hath he got
Against renownèd Douglas! Whose high deeds,   107
Whose hot incursions and great name in arms
Holds from all soldiers chief majority   109
And military title capital   110
Through all the kingdoms that acknowledge Christ.
Thrice hath this Hotspur, Mars in swaddling clothes,
This infant warrior, in his enterprises
Discomfited great Douglas, ta'en him once,   114
Enlargèd him and made a friend of him,   115
To fill the mouth of deep defiance up   116
And shake the peace and safety of our throne.
And what say you to this? Percy, Northumberland,
The Archbishop's Grace of York, Douglas, Mortimer,   119
Capitulate against us and are up.   120
But wherefore do I tell these news to thee?
Why, Harry, do I tell thee of my foes,
Which art my nearest and dearest enemy?   123

---

97 to boot in addition   **98–99 He . . . succession** i.e., even this rebel
Hotspur has a better claim to the throne than you, the mere shadow of
an heir   **100 of no right** having no rightful claim.   **color** pretext
101 harness armor, i.e., men in armor   **102 Turns head** leads an armed
insurrection.   **lion's** i.e., King's   **103 being . . . thou** i.e., being no older
than you (though historically Hotspur was twenty-three years older than
the Prince)   **107 Whose** i.e., Hotspur's   **109 majority** preeminence
110 capital chief, principal   **114 Discomfited** defeated   **115 Enlargèd**
freed   **116 To . . . up** i.e., to swell the roar of deep defiance   **119 The**
Archbishop's Grace i.e., His Grace the Archbishop   **120 Capitulate** form
a league, draw up articles.   **up** up in arms   **123 dearest** (1) most precious (2) direst

Thou that art like enough, through vassal fear,   124
Base inclination, and the start of spleen,   125
To fight against me under Percy's pay,
To dog his heels and curtsy at his frowns,
To show how much thou art degenerate.

PRINCE
Do not think so. You shall not find it so.
And God forgive them that so much have swayed
Your Majesty's good thoughts away from me!
I will redeem all this on Percy's head
And in the closing of some glorious day
Be bold to tell you that I am your son,
When I will wear a garment all of blood
And stain my favors in a bloody mask,   136
Which, washed away, shall scour my shame with it.
And that shall be the day, whene'er it lights,   138
That this same child of honor and renown,
This gallant Hotspur, this all-praisèd knight,
And your unthought-of Harry chance to meet.   141
For every honor sitting on his helm,
Would they were multitudes, and on my head
My shames redoubled! For the time will come
That I shall make this northern youth exchange
His glorious deeds for my indignities.
Percy is but my factor, good my lord,   147
To engross up glorious deeds on my behalf;   148
And I will call him to so strict account
That he shall render every glory up,
Yea, even the slightest worship of his time,   151
Or I will tear the reckoning from his heart.
This in the name of God I promise here,
The which if He be pleased I shall perform,
I do beseech Your Majesty may salve   155
The long-grown wounds of my intemperance.   156
If not, the end of life cancels all bonds,

---

124 like likely.   **vassal** slavish   **125 Base inclination** inclination for
baseness.   **start of spleen** fit of ill temper   **136 favors** features
138 lights dawns   **141 unthought-of** ignored, disregarded   **147 factor**
agent   **148 engross** amass, buy up   **151 worship of his time** honor of
his youthful lifetime   **155 salve** soothe, heal   **156 intemperance** disso-
lute living, sickness

And I will die a hundred thousand deaths
Ere break the smallest parcel of this vow.

KING
A hundred thousand rebels die in this!
Thou shalt have charge and sovereign trust herein.   161

    Enter Blunt.

How now, good Blunt? Thy looks are full of speed.

BLUNT
So hath the business that I come to speak of.
Lord Mortimer of Scotland hath sent word   164
That Douglas and the English rebels met
The eleventh of this month at Shrewsbury.
A mighty and a fearful head they are,   167
If promises be kept on every hand,
As ever offered foul play in a state.

KING
The Earl of Westmorland set forth today,
With him my son, Lord John of Lancaster;
For this advertisement is five days old.   172
On Wednesday next, Harry, you shall set forward;
On Thursday we ourselves will march. Our meeting   174
Is Bridgnorth. And, Harry, you shall march   175
Through Gloucestershire; by which account,
Our business valuèd, some twelve days hence   177
Our general forces at Bridgnorth shall meet.
Our hands are full of business. Let's away!
Advantage feeds him fat while men delay.   *Exeunt.* 180

❖

3.3   *Enter Falstaff and Bardolph.*

FALSTAFF   Bardolph, am I not fallen away vilely since this 1

---

161 charge command (of troops) **164 Lord Mortimer of Scotland** (A
Scottish nobleman, unrelated to Glendower's son-in-law.) **167 A** i.e.,
as. **head** armed force **172 advertisement** tidings, news **174 meeting**
place of rendezvous **175 Bridgnorth** a town near Shrewsbury
177 Our business valuèd estimating how long our business will take
180 Advantage . . . fat opportunity (for rebellion) prospers

3.3. Location: A tavern in Eastcheap, as in 2.4.
1 fallen away shrunk

last action? Do I not bate? Do I not dwindle? Why, my 2
skin hangs about me like an old lady's loose gown; I
am withered like an old applejohn. Well, I'll repent, 4
and that suddenly, while I am in some liking. I shall 5
be out of heart shortly, and then I shall have no 6
strength to repent. An I have not forgotten what the 7
inside of a church is made of, I am a peppercorn, a 8
brewer's horse. The inside of a church! Company, vil- 9
lainous company, hath been the spoil of me.

BARDOLPH   Sir John, you are so fretful you cannot live 11
long.

FALSTAFF   Why, there is it. Come sing me a bawdy
song; make me merry. I was as virtuously given as a 14
gentleman need to be, virtuous enough: swore little,
diced not above seven times—a week, went to a
bawdy house not above once in a quarter—of an
hour, paid money that I borrowed—three or four
times, lived well and in good compass; and now I live 19
out of all order, out of all compass.

BARDOLPH   Why, you are so fat, Sir John, that you must
needs be out of all compass, out of all reasonable compass, Sir John.

FALSTAFF   Do thou amend thy face, and I'll amend my
life. Thou art our admiral, thou bearest the lantern in 25
the poop, but 'tis in the nose of thee. Thou art the
Knight of the Burning Lamp.

BARDOLPH   Why, Sir John, my face does you no harm.

FALSTAFF   No, I'll be sworn, I make as good use of it as
many a man doth of a death's-head or a *memento* 30
mori. I never see thy face but I think upon hellfire and 31
Dives that lived in purple; for there he is in his robes, 32

---

2 action i.e., the robbery at Gad's Hill. bate lose weight 4 applejohn a
kind of apple still in good eating condition when shriveled 5 liking
(1) good bodily condition (2) inclination 6 out of heart (1) disinclined,
disheartened (2) out of condition 7 An if 8 peppercorn unground
dried pepper berry 9 brewer's horse i.e., one that is old, withered, and
decrepit 11 fretful (1) anxious (2) fretted, frayed 14 given inclined
19 good compass reasonable limits; also, in Bardolph's speech, girth,
circumference 25 admiral flagship. lantern i.e., a light for the rest of
the fleet to follow; here applied to Bardolph's inflamed nose, red from
overdrinking 30–31 memento mori reminder of death, such as a
death's head or a skull engraved on a seal ring 32 Dives the rich man
who went to hell, referred to in Luke 16:19–31

burning, burning. If thou wert any way given to virtue, I would swear by thy face; my oath should be "By 34
this fire, that's God's angel." But thou art altogether 35
given over, and wert indeed, but for the light in thy 36
face, the son of utter darkness. When thou rann'st up
Gad's Hill in the night to catch my horse, if I did not
think thou hadst been an *ignis fatuus* or a ball of wild- 39
fire, there's no purchase in money. O, thou art a per- 40
petual triumph, an everlasting bonfire light! Thou 41
hast saved me a thousand marks in links and torches, 42
walking with thee in the night betwixt tavern and tavern; but the sack that thou hast drunk me would have
bought me lights as good cheap at the dearest chan- 45
dler's in Europe. I have maintained that salamander of 46
yours with fire any time this two-and-thirty years. God
reward me for it!

BARDOLPH 'Sblood, I would my face were in your belly! 49

FALSTAFF God-a-mercy! So should I be sure to be heart-
burned.

   Enter Hostess.

How now, Dame Partlet the hen? Have you inquired 52
yet who picked my pocket?

HOSTESS Why, Sir John, what do you think, Sir John?
Do you think I keep thieves in my house? I have
searched, I have inquired, so has my husband, man by
man, boy by boy, servant by servant. The tithe of a 57
hair was never lost in my house before.

FALSTAFF Ye lie, hostess. Bardolph was shaved and lost 59
many a hair; and I'll be sworn my pocket was picked. 60
Go to, you are a woman, go.

34–35 By . . . angel (A biblical echo, perhaps to Psalms 104:4,
Hebrews 1:7, or Exodus 3:2.) **36 given over** abandoned to wickedness
39 ignis fatuus will-o'-the-wisp **39–40 wildfire** fireworks; lightning;
will-o'-the-wisp **41 triumph** procession led by torches **42 links**
torches, flares **45 good cheap** cheap. **dearest** most expensive
45–46 chandler's candle maker's **46 salamander** lizard reputed to be
able to live in fire **49 I . . . belly** (A proverb meaning "I wish I were rid
of this irritation"; stock response to an insult based on physical deform-
ity.) **52 Partlet** (Traditional name of a hen.) **57 tithe** tenth part
59 was shaved (1) had his beard cut (2) was cheated and robbed
59–60 lost many a hair (1) was shaved (2) was made bald by syphilis

HOSTESS   Who, I? No, I defy thee! God's light, I was   62
never called so in mine own house before.

FALSTAFF   Go to, I know you well enough.

HOSTESS   No, Sir John, you do not know me, Sir John. I
know you, Sir John. You owe me money, Sir John,
and now you pick a quarrel to beguile me of it. I
bought you a dozen of shirts to your back.

FALSTAFF   Dowlas, filthy dowlas. I have given them   69
away to bakers' wives; they have made bolters of   70
them.

HOSTESS   Now, as I am a true woman, holland of eight   72
shillings an ell. You owe money here besides, Sir   73
John, for your diet and by-drinkings, and money lent   74
you, four-and-twenty pound.

FALSTAFF   He had his part of it. Let him pay.   76

HOSTESS   He? Alas, he is poor, he hath nothing.

FALSTAFF   How, poor? Look upon his face. What call
you rich? Let them coin his nose, let them coin his
cheeks. I'll not pay a denier. What, will you make a   80
younker of me? Shall I not take mine ease in mine inn   81
but I shall have my pocket picked? I have lost a seal
ring of my grandfather's worth forty mark.

HOSTESS   O Jesu, I have heard the Prince tell him, I
know not how oft, that that ring was copper!

FALSTAFF   How? The Prince is a Jack, a sneak-up.   86
'Sblood, an he were here, I would cudgel him like a
dog if he would say so.   88

> *Enter the Prince [with Peto], marching, and*
> *Falstaff meets him playing upon his truncheon*
> *like a fife.*

How now, lad, is the wind in that door, i' faith? Must   89
we all march?

BARDOLPH   Yea, two and two, Newgate fashion.   91

HOSTESS   My lord, I pray you, hear me.

---

62 God's light (A mild oath.)   **69 Dowlas** a coarse kind of linen
70 bolters cloths for sifting flour   **72 holland** fine linen   **73 an ell** a
measure of 45 inches   **74 diet** meals.   **by-drinkings** drinks between
meals   **76 He** i.e., Bardolph   **80 denier** one-twelfth of a French sou;
type of very small coin   **81 younker** i.e., greenhorn   **86 Jack** knave,
rascal.   **sneak-up** sneak   **88 s.d. truncheon** officer's staff   **89 is . . .
door** i.e., is that the way the wind is blowing   **91 Newgate** (A famous
city prison in London. Prisoners marched two by two.)

PRINCE   What sayst thou, Mistress Quickly? How doth
thy husband? I love him well; he is an honest man.

HOSTESS   Good my lord, hear me.

FALSTAFF   Prithee, let her alone and list to me.

PRINCE   What sayst thou, Jack?

FALSTAFF   The other night I fell asleep here behind the
arras and had my pocket picked. This house is turned
bawdy house; they pick pockets.

PRINCE   What didst thou lose, Jack?

FALSTAFF   Wilt thou believe me, Hal? Three or four
bonds of forty pound apiece, and a seal ring of my
grandfather's.

PRINCE   A trifle, some eightpenny matter.

HOSTESS   So I told him, my lord, and I said I heard Your
Grace say so; and, my lord, he speaks most vilely of
you, like a foulmouthed man as he is, and said he
would cudgel you.

PRINCE   What, he did not!

HOSTESS   There's neither faith, truth, nor womanhood
in me else.

FALSTAFF   There's no more faith in thee than in a stewed   113
prune, nor no more truth in thee than in a drawn fox;   114
and for womanhood, Maid Marian may be the dep-   115
uty's wife of the ward to thee. Go, you thing, go.   116

HOSTESS   Say, what thing, what thing?

FALSTAFF   What thing? Why, a thing to thank God on.   118

HOSTESS   I am no thing to thank God on, I would thou   119
shouldst know it! I am an honest man's wife, and, set-   120
ting thy knighthood aside, thou art a knave to call   121
me so.

FALSTAFF   Setting thy womanhood aside, thou art a   123
beast to say otherwise.

HOSTESS   Say, what beast, thou knave, thou?

FALSTAFF   What beast? Why, an otter.

113–114 stewed prune (Customarily associated with bawdy houses.)
114 drawn fox fox driven from cover and wily in getting back
115–116 Maid . . . thee i.e., Maid Marian, disreputable woman in Robin
Hood ballads, morris dances, and the like, was a model of respectability
compared with you   **118, 119 What thing . . . no thing** (with sexual
quibbles)   **120–121, 123 setting . . . aside** (Mistress Quickly means,
"without wishing to offend your rank of knighthood," but Falstaff
replies in l. 123 with the meaning, "setting aside your womanhood as of
no value or pertinence.")

PRINCE   An otter, Sir John! Why an otter?

FALSTAFF   Why? She's neither fish nor flesh; a man
knows not where to have her.   129

HOSTESS   Thou art an unjust man in saying so. Thou or
any man knows where to have me, thou knave, thou!

PRINCE   Thou sayst true, hostess, and he slanders thee
most grossly.

HOSTESS   So he doth you, my lord, and said this other
day you ought him a thousand pound.   135

PRINCE   Sirrah, do I owe you a thousand pound?

FALSTAFF   A thousand pound, Hal? A million. Thy love
is worth a million; thou owest me thy love.

HOSTESS   Nay, my lord, he called you Jack and said he
would cudgel you.

FALSTAFF   Did I, Bardolph?

BARDOLPH   Indeed, Sir John, you said so.

FALSTAFF   Yea, if he said my ring was copper.

PRINCE   I say 'tis copper. Darest thou be as good as thy
word now?

FALSTAFF   Why, Hal, thou knowest, as thou art but
man, I dare; but as thou art prince, I fear thee as I fear
the roaring of the lion's whelp.   148

PRINCE   And why not as the lion?

FALSTAFF   The King himself is to be feared as the lion.
Dost thou think I'll fear thee as I fear thy father? Nay,
an I do, I pray God my girdle break.

PRINCE   O, if it should, how would thy guts fall about
thy knees! But, sirrah, there's no room for faith, truth,
nor honesty in this bosom of thine; it is all filled up
with guts and midriff. Charge an honest woman with
picking thy pocket! Why, thou whoreson, impudent,
embossed rascal, if there were anything in thy pocket   158
but tavern reckonings, memorandums of bawdy   159
houses, and one poor pennyworth of sugar candy to
make thee long-winded, if thy pocket were enriched
with any other injuries but these, I am a villain. And   162

---

129 have understand (with suggestion of enjoying sexually)   **135 ought**
owed   **148 whelp** cub   **158 embossed** (1) swollen with fat (2) foaming at
the mouth and exhausted, like a hunted animal.   **rascal** (1) scoundrel
(2) immature and inferior deer   **159 memorandums** souvenirs   **162 injuries** i.e., those things you claim to have lost, thereby suffering harm

yet you will stand to it; you will not pocket up wrong! 163
Art thou not ashamed?

FALSTAFF   Dost thou hear, Hal? Thou knowest in the
state of innocency Adam fell; and what should poor
Jack Falstaff do in the days of villainy? Thou seest I
have more flesh than another man, and therefore more
frailty. You confess then you picked my pocket?

PRINCE   It appears so by the story.   170

FALSTAFF   Hostess, I forgive thee. Go make ready breakfast. Love thy husband, look to thy servants, cherish
thy guests. Thou shalt find me tractable to any honest
reason; thou seest I am pacified still. Nay, prithee, be- 174
gone. (*Exit Hostess*.) Now, Hal, to the news at court: for
the robbery, lad, how is that answered?

PRINCE   O my sweet beef, I must still be good angel to
thee. The money is paid back again.

FALSTAFF   O, I do not like that paying back. 'Tis a dou- 179
ble labor.   180

PRINCE   I am good friends with my father and may do
anything.

FALSTAFF   Rob me the exchequer the first thing thou
dost, and do it with unwashed hands too.   184

BARDOLPH   Do, my lord.

PRINCE   I have procured thee, Jack, a charge of foot.   186

FALSTAFF   I would it had been of horse. Where shall I
find one that can steal well? O, for a fine thief of the 188
age of two-and-twenty or thereabouts! I am heinously
unprovided. Well, God be thanked for these rebels; 190
they offend none but the virtuous. I laud them, I 191
praise them.

PRINCE   Bardolph!

BARDOLPH   My lord?

PRINCE
Go bear this letter to Lord John of Lancaster,

---

163 stand to it make a stand, insist on your supposed rights.   **pocket up** endure silently   **170 by** according to   **174 still** always
179–180 double labor i.e., the taking and the returning   **184 with unwashed hands** i.e., at once   **186 charge of foot** command of a company of infantry   **188 one** i.e., a companion in thievery. (Falstaff sees war as the opportunity for stealing and conning.)   **190 unprovided** ill-equipped   **191 they . . . virtuous** i.e., the rebels, by providing the occasion of war, give dishonest men a chance to profiteer and hence offend only those who are honest

To my brother John; this to my lord of Westmorland.
                    [*He gives letters. Exit Bardolph.*]
Go, Peto, to horse, to horse, for thou and I
Have thirty miles to ride yet ere dinnertime.
                                        [*Exit Peto.*]
Jack, meet me tomorrow in the Temple Hall   199
At two o'clock in the afternoon.
There shalt thou know thy charge, and there receive
Money and order for their furniture.   202
The land is burning. Percy stands on high,
And either we or they must lower lie.   [*Exit.*]

FALSTAFF
Rare words, brave world! Hostess, my breakfast, come! 205
O, I could wish this tavern were my drum!   [*Exit.*] 206

❖

199 Temple Hall i.e., at the Inner Temple, one of the Inns of Court
202 furniture equipment, furnishing   **205 brave** splendid   **206 drum**
(Possibly Falstaff means that he wishes he could continue to enjoy this
tavern instead of risking his life in battle. He may also be punning on
tavern/taborn, i.e., *taborin*, a kind of drum.)

4.1   [*Enter Hotspur, Worcester, and Douglas.*]

HOTSPUR
  Well said, my noble Scot. If speaking truth
  In this fine age were not thought flattery,
  Such attribution should the Douglas have   3
  As not a soldier of this season's stamp   4
  Should go so general current through the world.   5
  By God, I cannot flatter; I do defy   6
  The tongues of soothers! But a braver place   7
  In my heart's love hath no man than yourself.
  Nay, task me to my word; approve me, lord.   9
DOUGLAS   Thou art the king of honor.
  No man so potent breathes upon the ground
  But I will beard him.

         Enter one [a Messenger] with letters.

HOTSPUR   Do so, and 'tis well.—   12
  What letters hast thou there?—I can but thank you.
MESSENGER
  These letters come from your father.
HOTSPUR
  Letters from him? Why comes he not himself?
MESSENGER
  He cannot come, my lord. He is grievous sick.
HOTSPUR
  Zounds, how has he the leisure to be sick
  In such a jostling time? Who leads his power?   18
  Under whose government come they along?   19
MESSENGER
  His letters bears his mind, not I, my lord.
                            [*Hotspur reads the letter.*]

4.1. Location: The rebel camp near Shrewsbury.
3 attribution praise, tribute   **4 stamp** coinage   **5 go ... current** be so
widely accepted and acclaimed. (Continues the metaphor of coinage.)
6 defy proclaim against   **7 soothers** flatterers.   **braver** better, dearer
9 task ... word challenge me to make good my word.   **approve** test
12 But ... him but that I will defy him   **18 jostling** contending, clash-
ing   **19 government** command

WORCESTER
  I prithee, tell me, doth he keep his bed?   21
MESSENGER
  He did, my lord, four days ere I set forth,
  And at the time of my departure thence
  He was much feared by his physicians.   24
WORCESTER
  I would the state of time had first been whole   25
  Ere he by sickness had been visited.
  His health was never better worth than now.
HOTSPUR
  Sick now? Droop now? This sickness doth infect
  The very life-blood of our enterprise;
  'Tis catching hither, even to our camp.
  He writes me here that inward sickness—
  And that his friends by deputation   32
  Could not so soon be drawn, nor did he think it meet 33
  To lay so dangerous and dear a trust
  On any soul removed but on his own.   35
  Yet doth he give us bold advertisement   36
  That with our small conjunction we should on,   37
  To see how fortune is disposed to us;
  For, as he writes, there is no quailing now,   39
  Because the King is certainly possessed   40
  Of all our purposes. What say you to it?
WORCESTER
  Your father's sickness is a maim to us.   42
HOTSPUR
  A perilous gash, a very limb lopped off.
  And yet, in faith, it is not! His present want   44
  Seems more than we shall find it. Were it good   45
  To set the exact wealth of all our states   46
  All at one cast? To set so rich a main   47
  On the nice hazard of one doubtful hour?   48

21 keep keep to, stay in **24 feared** feared for **25 time** the times **32 by deputation** through deputies **33 drawn** assembled. **meet** appropriate **35 On . . . own** on anyone other than himself **36 advertisement** counsel, advice **37 conjunction** joint force. **on** go on **39 quailing** losing heart **40 possessed** informed **42 maim** injury **44 want** absence **45 more** more serious **46 To . . . states** to stake the absolute total of our resources **47 cast** throw of the dice. **main** stake in gambling; also, an army **48 nice** precarious, delicate. **hazard** (1) game at dice (2) venture

It were not good, for therein should we read   49
The very bottom and the soul of hope,   50
The very list, the very utmost bound   51
Of all our fortunes.

DOUGLAS   Faith, and so we should;
Where now remains a sweet reversion,   53
We may boldly spend upon the hope
Of what is to come in.
A comfort of retirement lives in this.   56

HOTSPUR
A rendezvous, a home to fly unto,
If that the devil and mischance look big   58
Upon the maidenhead of our affairs.   59

WORCESTER
But yet I would your father had been here.
The quality and hair of our attempt   61
Brooks no division. It will be thought   62
By some that know not why he is away
That wisdom, loyalty, and mere dislike   64
Of our proceedings kept the Earl from hence.
And think how such an apprehension   66
May turn the tide of fearful faction   67
And breed a kind of question in our cause.
For well you know we of the offering side   69
Must keep aloof from strict arbitrament,   70
And stop all sight holes, every loop from whence   71
The eye of reason may pry in upon us.
This absence of your father's draws a curtain   73
That shows the ignorant a kind of fear
Before not dreamt of.

HOTSPUR   You strain too far.   75
I rather of his absence make this use:
It lends a luster and more great opinion,   77

49–50 should . . . hope we should discover the utmost foundation and
basis of our hopes, the most we could rely on   **51 list** limit
53 reversion (Literally, part of an estate yet to be inherited.)
56 retirement something to fall back on   **58 big** threatening
59 maidenhead i.e., commencement   **61 hair** kind, nature   **62 Brooks**
tolerates   **64 loyalty** i.e., to the crown.   **mere** absolute
66 apprehension (1) perception (2) apprehensiveness   **67 fearful faction**
timid support   **69 offering side** side that attacks   **70 strict arbitrament**
just inquiry or investigation   **71 loop** loophole   **73 draws** draws aside,
opens   **75 strain too far** exaggerate   **77 opinion** renown

A larger dare to our great enterprise,
Than if the Earl were here; for men must think,
If we without his help can make a head   80
To push against a kingdom, with his help
We shall o'erturn it topsy-turvy down.
Yet all goes well, yet all our joints are whole.   83

DOUGLAS
As heart can think. There is not such a word
Spoke of in Scotland as this term of fear.

Enter Sir Richard Vernon.

HOTSPUR
My cousin Vernon, welcome, by my soul.

VERNON
Pray God my news be worth a welcome, lord.
The Earl of Westmorland, seven thousand strong,
Is marching hitherwards; with him Prince John.

HOTSPUR
No harm. What more?

VERNON   And further I have learned
The King himself in person is set forth,
Or hitherwards intended speedily,   92
With strong and mighty preparation.

HOTSPUR
He shall be welcome too. Where is his son,
The nimble-footed madcap Prince of Wales,
And his comrades, that doffed the world aside   96
And bid it pass?

VERNON   All furnished, all in arms;   97
All plumed like estridges, that with the wind   98
Bated like eagles having lately bathed,   99
Glittering in golden coats, like images,   100
As full of spirit as the month of May
And gorgeous as the sun at midsummer,
Wanton as youthful goats, wild as young bulls.   103
I saw young Harry, with his beaver on,   104

80 make a head raise an armed force **83 Yet** still. **joints** limbs
92 intended on the verge of departure **96 doffed** put aside with a gesture **97 furnished** equipped **98 estridges** ostriches. (Refers to ostrich
plumes on crests.) **99 Bated** flapped their wings. (From falconry.)
100 coats (1) coats of mail (2) heraldic coats of arms. **images** gilded
statues **103 Wanton** sportive, frolicsome **104 beaver** visor; hence, helmet

His cuisses on his thighs, gallantly armed,   105
Rise from the ground like feathered Mercury,
And vaulted with such ease into his seat   107
As if an angel dropped down from the clouds
To turn and wind a fiery Pegasus   109
And witch the world with noble horsemanship.   110

HOTSPUR
No more, no more! Worse than the sun in March   111
This praise doth nourish agues. Let them come.   112
They come like sacrifices in their trim,   113
And to the fire-eyed maid of smoky war   114
All hot and bleeding will we offer them.
The mailèd Mars shall on his altar sit   116
Up to the ears in blood. I am on fire
To hear this rich reprisal is so nigh,   118
And yet not ours. Come, let me taste my horse,
Who is to bear me like a thunderbolt
Against the bosom of the Prince of Wales.
Harry to Harry shall, hot horse to horse,
Meet and ne'er part till one drop down a corse.
O, that Glendower were come!

VERNON   There is more news:
I learned in Worcester, as I rode along,
He cannot draw his power this fourteen days.   126

DOUGLAS
That's the worst tidings that I hear of yet.

WORCESTER
Ay, by my faith, that bears a frosty sound.

HOTSPUR
What may the King's whole battle reach unto?   129

VERNON
To thirty thousand.

HOTSPUR   Forty let it be!
My father and Glendower being both away,
The powers of us may serve so great a day.   132

---

105 cuisses armor for the thighs   **107 seat** i.e., saddle   **109 wind** wheel.
Pegasus winged horse of Greek mythology   **110 witch** bewitch
111–112 Worse . . . agues (The spring sun was believed to give impetus to
chills and fevers, by drawing up vapors.)   **113 sacrifices** beasts for sacri-
fice.   **trim** fine apparel, trappings   **114 maid** i.e., Bellona, goddess of war
116 mailèd dressed in mail, armor   **118 reprisal** prize   **126 draw his
power** muster his army   **129 battle** army   **132 The . . . us** our forces

Come, let us take a muster speedily.
Doomsday is near; die all, die merrily.

DOUGLAS
Talk not of dying. I am out of fear   135
Of death or death's hand for this one half year.

                                        Exeunt.

❖

4.2   *Enter Falstaff, [and] Bardolph.*

FALSTAFF   Bardolph, get thee before to Coventry; fill me
a bottle of sack. Our soldiers shall march through; we'll
to Sutton Coldfield tonight.   3

BARDOLPH   Will you give me money, Captain?

FALSTAFF   Lay out, lay out.   5

BARDOLPH   This bottle makes an angel.   6

FALSTAFF   An if it do, take it for thy labor; an if it make 7
twenty, take them all; I'll answer the coinage. Bid my 8
lieutenant Peto meet me at town's end.

BARDOLPH   I will, Captain. Farewell.   *Exit.*

FALSTAFF   If I be not ashamed of my soldiers, I am a
soused gurnet. I have misused the King's press dam-   12
nably. I have got, in exchange of a hundred and fifty
soldiers, three hundred and odd pounds. I press me   14
none but good householders, yeomen's sons, inquire   15
me out contracted bachelors, such as had been asked   16
twice on the banns—such a commodity of warm   17
slaves as had as lief hear the devil as a drum, such as 18
fear the report of a caliver worse than a struck fowl or 19

---

135 out of free from

4.2. Location: A public road near Coventry.
3 Sutton Coldfield (In Warwickshire near Coventry.)   **5 Lay out** i.e., pay
for it yourself   **6 makes an angel** i.e., makes 10 shillings I've spent for
you. (But Falstaff answers as though *makes* means "produces," imply-
ing that Bardolph has profited from the transaction.)   **7 An if** if
8 answer be responsible for.   **the coinage** i.e., the money produced
12 soused gurnet a kind of pickled fish.   **King's press** royal warrant for
the impressment of troops   **14 press me** draft, conscript   **15 good** i.e.,
wealthy.   **yeomen's** small freeholders'   **16 contracted** engaged to be
married   **17 banns** public announcements, declared on three Sundays
in succession, of an intent to marry.   **warm** i.e., loving their comfort
18 lief willingly   **19 caliver** musket.   **struck** wounded

a hurt wild duck. I pressed me none but such toasts- 20
and-butter, with hearts in their bellies no bigger than 21
pins' heads, and they have bought out their services; 22
and now my whole charge consists of ancients, cor- 23
porals, lieutenants, gentlemen of companies—slaves 24
as ragged as Lazarus in the painted cloth, where the 25
glutton's dogs licked his sores, and such as indeed
were never soldiers, but discarded unjust servingmen, 27
younger sons to younger brothers, revolted tapsters, 28
and hostlers trade-fallen, the cankers of a calm world 29
and a long peace, ten times more dishonorable-ragged
than an old feazed ancient. And such have I, to fill up 31
the rooms of them as have bought out their services,
that you would think that I had a hundred and fifty tat-
tered prodigals lately come from swine keeping, from 34
eating draff and husks. A mad fellow met me on the way 35
and told me I had unloaded all the gibbets and pressed 36
the dead bodies. No eye hath seen such scarecrows. I'll
not march through Coventry with them, that's flat. 38
Nay, and the villains march wide betwixt the legs as
if they had gyves on, for indeed I had the most of them 40
out of prison. There's not a shirt and a half in all my
company, and the half shirt is two napkins tacked together and thrown over the shoulders like a herald's
coat without sleeves; and the shirt, to say the truth,
stolen from my host at Saint Albans, or the red-nose 45
innkeeper of Daventry. But that's all one; they'll find 46
linen enough on every hedge. 47

Enter the Prince [and the] Lord of Westmorland.

20–21 toasts-and-butter weaklings **22 bought . . . services** i.e., paid,
bribed, to be released from military duty **23 charge** company, troop.
ancients ensigns, standard-bearers. (By appointing a disproportionate
number of junior officers, Falstaff has made it possible to collect for
himself their more substantial pay.) **24 gentlemen of companies** a kind
of junior officer **25 painted cloth** cheap hangings for a room. (For the
story of Lazarus the beggar and Dives the rich man, see Luke 16:19–31.)
27 unjust dishonest **28 younger . . . brothers** (i.e., with no possibility of
inheritance). **revolted** runaway **29 trade-fallen** whose business has
fallen away. **cankers** cankerworms that destroy leaves and buds. (Used
figuratively.) **31 feazed ancient** frayed flag **34 prodigals** (See
Luke 15:15–16.) **35 draff** hogwash **36 gibbets** gallows **38 that's flat**
that's for sure **40 gyves** fetters **45, 46 Saint Albans, Daventry** (Towns
north and west of London, on the road to Coventry.) **46 that's all one** no
matter **47 hedge** (Where wet linen was spread out to dry.)

PRINCE How now, blown Jack? How now, quilt?   48
FALSTAFF What, Hal? How now, mad wag? What a
devil dost thou in Warwickshire? My good lord of
Westmorland, I cry you mercy. I thought your honor 51
had already been at Shrewsbury.
WESTMORLAND Faith, Sir John, 'tis more than time that
I were there, and you too; but my powers are there 54
already. The King, I can tell you, looks for us all. We
must away all night.   56
FALSTAFF Tut, never fear me. I am as vigilant as a cat to 57
steal cream.
PRINCE I think, to steal cream indeed, for thy theft hath 59
already made thee butter. But tell me, Jack, whose fel- 60
lows are these that come after?
FALSTAFF Mine, Hal, mine.
PRINCE I did never see such pitiful rascals.
FALSTAFF Tut, tut, good enough to toss; food for pow- 64
der, food for powder. They'll fill a pit as well as better. 65
Tush, man, mortal men, mortal men.
WESTMORLAND Ay, but, Sir John, methinks they are ex-
ceeding poor and bare, too beggarly.
FALSTAFF Faith, for their poverty, I know not where 69
they had that, and for their bareness, I am sure they
never learned that of me.
PRINCE No, I'll be sworn, unless you call three fingers 72
in the ribs bare. But, sirrah, make haste. Percy is al- 73
ready in the field.   *Exit.*
FALSTAFF What, is the King encamped?
WESTMORLAND He is, Sir John. I fear we shall stay too
long.   [*Exit.*]
FALSTAFF Well,
To the latter end of a fray and the beginning of a feast
Fits a dull fighter and a keen guest.   *Exit.* 81

✣

48 blown swollen, inflated; also, short of wind **51 cry you mercy** beg
your pardon **54 powers** soldiers **56 must away** must march **57 fear**
worry about **59–60 thy . . . butter** i.e., all the cream (rich things) you
have stolen has been churned into butterfat in your barrel-like belly
64 toss i.e., on a pike **64–65 food for powder** cannon fodder **69 for** as
for **72–73 three . . . ribs** i.e., Falstaff's fat-covered ribs. (A *finger* was a
measure of three-fourths of an inch.) **81 keen** with keen appetite

4.3   *Enter Hotspur, Worcester, Douglas, [and]*
          Vernon.

HOTSPUR
  We'll fight with him tonight.
WORCESTER   It may not be.
DOUGLAS
  You give him then advantage.
VERNON   Not a whit.   2
HOTSPUR
  Why say you so? Looks he not for supply?   3
VERNON
  So do we.
HOTSPUR   His is certain; ours is doubtful.
WORCESTER
  Good cousin, be advised, stir not tonight.
VERNON
  Do not, my lord.
DOUGLAS   You do not counsel well.
  You speak it out of fear and cold heart.
VERNON
  Do me no slander, Douglas. By my life,
  And I dare well maintain it with my life,
  If well-respected honor bid me on,   10
  I hold as little counsel with weak fear
  As you, my lord, or any Scot that this day lives.
  Let it be seen tomorrow in the battle
  Which of us fears.
DOUGLAS   Yea, or tonight.
VERNON   Content.
HOTSPUR   Tonight, say I.
VERNON
  Come, come, it may not be. I wonder much,
  Being men of such great leading as you are,   19
  That you foresee not what impediments
  Drag back our expedition. Certain horse   21
  Of my cousin Vernon's are not yet come up.

4.3. Location: The rebel camp near Shrewsbury.
2 then i.e., if you wait. (Addressed to Worcester, not Hotspur.)   **3 supply**
reinforcements   **10 well-respected** well weighed or considered
19 leading leadership   **21 expedition** speedy progress.   **horse** cavalry
(as also in l. 23)

Your uncle Worcester's horse came but today,
And now their pride and mettle is asleep,   24
Their courage with hard labor tame and dull,
That not a horse is half the half of himself.

HOTSPUR
So are the horses of the enemy
In general journey-bated and brought low.   28
The better part of ours are full of rest.

WORCESTER
The number of the King exceedeth ours.
For God's sake, cousin, stay till all come in.   31

The trumpet sounds a parley.

Enter Sir Walter Blunt.

BLUNT
I come with gracious offers from the King,
If you vouchsafe me hearing and respect.   33

HOTSPUR
Welcome, Sir Walter Blunt; and would to God
You were of our determination!   35
Some of us love you well; and even those some   36
Envy your great deservings and good name
Because you are not of our quality   38
But stand against us like an enemy.

BLUNT
And God defend but still I should stand so,   40
So long as out of limit and true rule   41
You stand against anointed majesty.
But to my charge. The King hath sent to know
The nature of your griefs and whereupon   44
You conjure from the breast of civil peace
Such bold hostility, teaching his duteous land
Audacious cruelty. If that the King
Have any way your good deserts forgot,
Which he confesseth to be manifold,
He bids you name your griefs, and with all speed

24 pride and mettle spirit   **28 journey-bated** tired from the journey
31 s.d. parley trumpet summons to a conference   **33 respect** attention
35 determination persuasion (in the fight)   **36 even those some** i.e.,
those same persons among us who love you   **38 quality** party
40 defend forbid.   **still** always   **41 limit** bounds of allegiance   **44 griefs**
grievances

You shall have your desires with interest
And pardon absolute for yourself and these
Herein misled by your suggestion.   53

HOTSPUR
The King is kind; and well we know the King
Knows at what time to promise, when to pay.
My father and my uncle and myself
Did give him that same royalty he wears,
And when he was not six-and-twenty strong,
Sick in the world's regard, wretched and low,
A poor unminded outlaw sneaking home,
My father gave him welcome to the shore;
And when he heard him swear and vow to God
He came but to be Duke of Lancaster,
To sue his livery and beg his peace   64
With tears of innocency and terms of zeal,
My father, in kind heart and pity moved,
Swore him assistance, and performed it too.
Now when the lords and barons of the realm
Perceived Northumberland did lean to him,
The more and less came in with cap and knee,   70
Met him in boroughs, cities, villages,
Attended him on bridges, stood in lanes,   72
Laid gifts before him, proffered him their oaths,
Gave him their heirs as pages, followed him   74
Even at the heels in golden multitudes   75
He presently, as greatness knows itself,   76
Steps me a little higher than his vow   77
Made to my father while his blood was poor   78
Upon the naked shore at Ravenspurgh,
And now, forsooth, takes on him to reform
Some certain edicts and some strait decrees   81
That lie too heavy on the commonwealth,

---

53 suggestion instigation   **64 sue his livery** sue as an heir come of age
for the delivery of his lands.   **beg his peace** i.e., request to be reconciled
to King Richard   **70 more and less** persons of all ranks.   **with . . . knee**
i.e., with cap in hand and with bended knee   **72 Attended** waited for.
stood in lanes stood row-deep along the roads   **74 Gave . . . heirs** i.e., to
serve him   **75 golden** (1) auspicious, celebrating (2) majestically attired   **76 knows itself** perceives its own strength   **77 Steps me** i.e.,
steps. (*Me* is used colloquially.)   **vow** i.e., Henry's vow to seek no more
than his inheritance   **78 blood** spirit, temper.   **poor** i.e., unambitious
81 strait strict

Cries out upon abuses, seems to weep
Over his country's wrongs; and by this face,   84
This seeming brow of justice, did he win
The hearts of all that he did angle for;
Proceeded further—cut me off the heads   87
Of all the favorites that the absent King
In deputation left behind him here,
When he was personal in the Irish war.   90

BLUNT
Tut, I came not to hear this.

HOTSPUR   Then to the point.
In short time after, he deposed the King,
Soon after that, deprived him of his life,
And in the neck of that tasked the whole state;   94
To make that worse, suffered his kinsman March—
Who is, if every owner were well placed,   96
Indeed his king—to be engaged in Wales,   97
There without ransom to lie forfeited;   98
Disgraced me in my happy victories,   99
Sought to entrap me by intelligence;   100
Rated mine uncle from the Council board;   101
In rage dismissed my father from the court;
Broke oath on oath, committed wrong on wrong,
And in conclusion drove us to seek out
This head of safety, and withal to pry   105
Into his title, the which we find
Too indirect for long continuance.

BLUNT
Shall I return this answer to the King?

HOTSPUR
Not so, Sir Walter. We'll withdraw awhile.
Go to the King; and let there be impawned   110
Some surety for a safe return again,
And in the morning early shall mine uncle
Bring him our purposes. And so farewell.   113

84 face show, pretense **87 cut me** i.e., cut **90 personal** physically, in
person **94 in . . . that** next, immediately after. **tasked** laid taxes
upon **96 if . . . placed** if every claimant were given his proper place
97 engaged held as hostage **98 lie forfeited** remain prisoner, unre-
claimed **99 Disgraced me** (by demanding the prisoners; see 1.3.23 ff.)
happy fortunate **100 intelligence** secret information, i.e., from spies
101 Rated scolded **105 head of safety** armed force for our protection. **withal** also **110 impawned** pledged **113 purposes** proposals

BLUNT
   I would you would accept of grace and love.
HOTSPUR
   And maybe so we shall.
BLUNT   Pray God you do.   [*Exeunt.*]

❧

4.4   *Enter [the] Archbishop of York, [and] Sir*
            Michael.

ARCHBISHOP [*Giving letters*]
   Hie, good Sir Michael, bear this sealèd brief   1
   With wingèd haste to the Lord Marshal,   2
   This to my cousin Scroop, and all the rest   3
   To whom they are directed. If you knew
   How much they do import, you would make haste.
SIR MICHAEL   My good lord, I guess their tenor.
ARCHBISHOP   Like enough you do.
   Tomorrow, good Sir Michael, is a day
   Wherein the fortune of ten thousand men
   Must bide the touch; for, sir, at Shrewsbury,   10
   As I am truly given to understand,
   The King with mighty and quick-raisèd power
   Meets with Lord Harry. And I fear, Sir Michael,
   What with the sickness of Northumberland,
   Whose power was in the first proportion,   15
   And what with Owen Glendower's absence thence,
   Who with them was a rated sinew too   17
   And comes not in, o'erruled by prophecies,
   I fear the power of Percy is too weak
   To wage an instant trial with the King.   20
SIR MICHAEL
   Why, my good lord, you need not fear;
   There is Douglas and Lord Mortimer.

4.4. Location: York. The Archbishop's palace.
1 brief letter, dispatch   **2 Lord Marshal** i.e., Thomas Mowbray, son of
the Duke of Norfolk who is exiled in *Richard II*, and a longtime enemy
of the new King   **3 Scroop** i.e., perhaps Sir Stephen Scroop of *Richard
II*, 3.2.91–218, or Lord Scroop of Masham of *Henry V*, 2.2   **10 bide the
touch** be put to the test (like gold)   **15 in . . . proportion** of the largest
size   **17 rated sinew** main strength or support reckoned upon
20 instant immediate

ARCHBISHOP   No, Mortimer is not there.

SIR MICHAEL
  But there is Mordake, Vernon, Lord Harry Percy,
  And there is my lord of Worcester, and a head   25
  Of gallant warriors, noble gentlemen.

ARCHBISHOP
  And so there is. But yet the King hath drawn
  The special head of all the land together: 28
  The Prince of Wales, Lord John of Lancaster,
  The noble Westmorland, and warlike Blunt,
  And many more corrivals and dear men   31
  Of estimation and command in arms.   32

SIR MICHAEL
  Doubt not, my lord, they shall be well opposed.

ARCHBISHOP
  I hope no less, yet needful 'tis to fear;
  And, to prevent the worst, Sir Michael, speed.
  For if Lord Percy thrive not, ere the King
  Dismiss his power he means to visit us,   37
  For he hath heard of our confederacy,
  And 'tis but wisdom to make strong against him.
  Therefore make haste. I must go write again
  To other friends; and so farewell, Sir Michael.

                                        Exeunt.

                         ❖

---

25 head troop   **28 special head** notable leaders   **31 corrivals** partners
in the enterprise   **32 estimation** reputation, importance   **37 he** i.e., the
King

5.1   *Enter the King, Prince of Wales, Lord John of
Lancaster, Sir Walter Blunt, [and] Falstaff.*

KING
How bloodily the sun begins to peer
Above yon bosky hill! The day looks pale   2
At his distemperature.
PRINCE   The southern wind   3
Doth play the trumpet to his purposes,   4
And by his hollow whistling in the leaves
Foretells a tempest and a blustering day.
KING
Then with the losers let it sympathize,
For nothing can seem foul to those that win.

                                       The trumpet sounds.

       Enter Worcester [and Vernon].

How now, my lord of Worcester? 'Tis not well
That you and I should meet upon such terms
As now we meet. You have deceived our trust
And made us doff our easy robes of peace   12
To crush our old limbs in ungentle steel.
This is not well, my lord, this is not well.
What say you to it? Will you again unknit
This churlish knot of all-abhorrèd war
And move in that obedient orb again   17
Where you did give a fair and natural light,
And be no more an exhaled meteor,   19
A prodigy of fear, and a portent   20
Of broachèd mischief to the unborn times?   21
WORCESTER   Hear me, my liege:
For mine own part, I could be well content

5.1. Location: The King's camp near Shrewsbury.
2 bosky bushy   **3 his distemperature** i.e., the sun's unhealthy appearance   **4 trumpet** trumpeter.   **his** its, the sun's   **12 easy** comfortable
17 orb orbit, sphere of action. (The King's subjects, like planets and
stars in the Ptolemaic cosmos, were supposed to revolve around the
kingly center, comparable to the earth, in fixed courses.)   **19 exhaled
meteor** (Meteors were believed to be vapors drawn up or *exhaled* by the
sun and visible as streaks of light; they were regarded as ill omens.)
20 prodigy of fear fearful omen   **21 broachèd** set flowing, already begun

To entertain the lag end of my life   24
With quiet hours, for I protest
I have not sought the day of this dislike.   26

KING
You have not sought it? How comes it, then?

FALSTAFF   Rebellion lay in his way, and he found it.

PRINCE   Peace, chewet, peace!   29

WORCESTER
It pleased Your Majesty to turn your looks
Of favor from myself and all our house;
And yet I must remember you, my lord,   32
We were the first and dearest of your friends.
For you my staff of office did I break
In Richard's time, and posted day and night   35
To meet you on the way, and kiss your hand,
When yet you were in place and in account
Nothing so strong and fortunate as I.   38
It was myself, my brother, and his son
That brought you home and boldly did outdare   40
The dangers of the time. You swore to us,
And you did swear that oath at Doncaster,
That you did nothing purpose 'gainst the state,
Nor claim no further than your new-fall'n right,   44
The seat of Gaunt, dukedom of Lancaster.
To this we swore our aid. But in short space
It rained down fortune showering on your head,
And such a flood of greatness fell on you—
What with our help, what with the absent King,
What with the injuries of a wanton time,   50
The seeming sufferances that you had borne,   51
And the contrarious winds that held the King
So long in his unlucky Irish wars
That all in England did repute him dead—
And from this swarm of fair advantages
You took occasion to be quickly wooed   56

---

24 entertain occupy   **26 the . . . dislike** this time of discord   **29 chewet**
chough, jackdaw. (Here, a chatterer.)   **32 remember** remind   **35 posted**
rode swiftly   **38 Nothing** not at all   **40 brought** escorted   **44 new-fall'n**
recently inherited (by the death of John of Gaunt)   **50 injuries** abuses,
evils.   **wanton** lawless   **51 sufferances** suffering, distress   **56 occasion**
the opportunity

To grip the general sway into your hand;
Forgot your oath to us at Doncaster;
And being fed by us, you used us so
As that ungentle gull, the cuckoo's bird,   60
Useth the sparrow; did oppress our nest,
Grew by our feeding to so great a bulk
That even our love durst not come near your sight   63
For fear of swallowing; but with nimble wing
We were enforced, for safety's sake, to fly
Out of your sight and raise this present head,   66
Whereby we stand opposèd by such means   67
As you yourself have forged against yourself
By unkind usage, dangerous countenance,   69
And violation of all faith and troth
Sworn to us in your younger enterprise.

KING

These things indeed you have articulate,   72
Proclaimed at market crosses, read in churches,
To face the garment of rebellion   74
With some fine color that may please the eye   75
Of fickle changelings and poor discontents,   76
Which gape and rub the elbow at the news   77
Of hurly-burly innovation.   78
And never yet did insurrection want   79
Such water-colors to impaint his cause,   80
Nor moody beggars, starving for a time   81
Of pell-mell havoc and confusion.   82

PRINCE

In both your armies there is many a soul   83
Shall pay full dearly for this encounter,
If once they join in trial. Tell your nephew
The Prince of Wales doth join with all the world

---

60 ungentle gull rude young bird, still unfledged.   **cuckoo's bird** cuckoo's young offspring. (The cuckoo lays its eggs in other birds' nests.)
63 our love we in our love   **66 head** armed force   **67 opposèd . . . means** goaded into opposition by such factors   **69 dangerous countenance** threatening behavior   **72 articulate** set forth, specified   **74 face** trim, adorn   **75 color** (1) hue (2) specious appearance   **76 changelings** turncoats   **77 rub the elbow** i.e., hug themselves with delight
78 innovation rebellion   **79 want** lack   **80 water-colors** i.e., thin excuses. (See *color*, l. 75.)   **his** its   **81 moody** sullen, angry   **82 havoc** plundering   **83 both your** i.e., your and our

In praise of Henry Percy. By my hopes—   87
This present enterprise set off his head—   88
I do not think a braver gentleman,
More active-valiant or more valiant-young,
More daring or more bold, is now alive
To grace this latter age with noble deeds.
For my part, I may speak it to my shame,
I have a truant been to chivalry;
And so I hear he doth account me too.
Yet this before my father's majesty:
I am content that he shall take the odds
Of his great name and estimation,   98
And will, to save the blood on either side,
Try fortune with him in a single fight.

KING
And, Prince of Wales, so dare we venture thee,   101
Albeit considerations infinite   102
Do make against it. No, good Worcester, no,
We love our people well; even those we love
That are misled upon your cousin's part.
And, will they take the offer of our grace,   106
Both he and they and you, yea, every man
Shall be my friend again, and I'll be his.
So tell your cousin, and bring me word
What he will do. But if he will not yield,
Rebuke and dread correction wait on us,   111
And they shall do their office. So, begone.
We will not now be troubled with reply.
We offer fair; take it advisedly.
                    Exeunt Worcester [and Vernon].

PRINCE
It will not be accepted, on my life.
The Douglas and the Hotspur both together
Are confident against the world in arms.

KING
Hence, therefore, every leader to his charge;
For on their answer will we set on them,

---

87 hopes i.e., hopes of salvation   **88 This . . . head** i.e., if this present
rebellion is taken from his account, not held against him   **98 estimation**
reputation   **101 venture** hazard, risk   **102 Albeit** although it be that.
(The subjunctive has the force of "were it not that.")   **106 grace** pardon   **111 wait on us** are in attendance upon us

And God befriend us as our cause is just!   120
                    Exeunt. Manent Prince, Falstaff.

FALSTAFF Hal, if thou see me down in the battle and
  bestride me, so; 'tis a point of friendship.   122

PRINCE Nothing but a colossus can do thee that friendship. Say thy prayers, and farewell.

FALSTAFF I would 'twere bedtime, Hal, and all well.

PRINCE Why, thou owest God a death.   [*Exit.*] 126

FALSTAFF 'Tis not due yet; I would be loath to pay him
  before his day. What need I be so forward with him
  that calls not on me? Well, 'tis no matter; honor pricks 129
  me on. Yea, but how if honor prick me off when I 130
  come on? How then? Can honor set to a leg? No. Or 131
  an arm? No. Or take away the grief of a wound? No. 132
  Honor hath no skill in surgery, then? No. What is
  honor? A word. What is in that word "honor"? What is
  that "honor"? Air. A trim reckoning! Who hath it? He
  that died o' Wednesday. Doth he feel it? No. Doth he
  hear it? No. 'Tis insensible, then? Yea, to the dead. But
  will it not live with the living? No. Why? Detraction 138
  will not suffer it. Therefore I'll none of it. Honor is a 139
  mere scutcheon. And so ends my catechism.   140
                              Exit.

❖

5.2   *Enter Worcester, [and] Sir Richard Vernon.*

WORCESTER
  O, no, my nephew must not know, Sir Richard,
  The liberal and kind offer of the King.

VERNON
  'Twere best he did.

WORCESTER   Then are we all undone.
  It is not possible, it cannot be,

120 s.d. Manent they remain onstage   **122 so** well and good   **126 thou
. . . death** (Proverbial, with a pun on *debt*.)   **129 pricks** spurs   **130 prick
me off** mark me off (as one dead)   **131 set to** rejoin or set   **132 grief**
pain   **138 Detraction** slander   **139 suffer** allow   **140 scutcheon** heraldic emblem carried in funerals, displayed on coaches, etc.; it was the
lowest form of symbol, having no pennon or other insignia.   **catechism**
the principles of faith given in the form of question and answer

5.2 Location: Near the rebel camp.

The King should keep his word in loving us;
He will suspect us still and find a time
To punish this offense in other faults.   7
Suspicion all our lives shall be stuck full of eyes;   8
For treason is but trusted like the fox,
Who, never so tame, so cherished, and locked up,   10
Will have a wild trick of his ancestors.   11
Look how we can, or sad or merrily,   12
Interpretation will misquote our looks,
And we shall feed like oxen at a stall,
The better cherished still the nearer death.
My nephew's trespass may be well forgot;
It hath the excuse of youth and heat of blood,
And an adopted name of privilege,   18
A harebrained Hotspur, governed by a spleen.   19
All his offenses live upon my head
And on his father's. We did train him on,   21
And, his corruption being ta'en from us,   22
We as the spring of all shall pay for all.   23
Therefore, good cousin, let not Harry know
In any case the offer of the King.

        Enter Hotspur [and Douglas, with soldiers].

VERNON
    Deliver what you will; I'll say 'tis so.   26
    Here comes your cousin.
HOTSPUR   My uncle is returned.
    Deliver up my lord of Westmorland.   28
    Uncle, what news?
WORCESTER
    The King will bid you battle presently.
DOUGLAS
    Defy him by the lord of Westmorland.   31
HOTSPUR
    Lord Douglas, go you and tell him so.

7 in in punishing   **8 stuck . . . eyes** i.e., provided with many eyes, suspi-
ciously inquisitive   **10 never so** be he never so   **11 trick** trait   **12 or
sad** either sad   **18 adopted . . . privilege** i.e., a nickname, "hotspur," to
justify his rashness   **19 spleen** intemperate impulse   **21 train** incite,
draw   **22 his . . . us** i.e., since his guilt originated in us   **23 spring**
source   **26 Deliver** report   **28 Deliver up** release (as hostage; see
4.3.110–111)   **31 Defy him by** send back your defiance with

DOUGLAS
  Marry, and shall, and very willingly.   *Exit Douglas.*

WORCESTER
  There is no seeming mercy in the King.

HOTSPUR
  Did you beg any? God forbid!

WORCESTER
  I told him gently of our grievances,
  Of his oath breaking, which he mended thus,
  By now forswearing that he is forsworn.
  He calls us rebels, traitors, and will scourge
  With haughty arms this hateful name in us.

    Enter Douglas.

DOUGLAS
  Arm, gentlemen, to arms! For I have thrown
  A brave defiance in King Henry's teeth,   42
  And Westmorland, that was engaged, did bear it;   43
  Which cannot choose but bring him quickly on.

WORCESTER
  The Prince of Wales stepped forth before the King,
  And, nephew, challenged you to single fight.

HOTSPUR
  O, would the quarrel lay upon our heads,
  And that no man might draw short breath today
  But I and Harry Monmouth! Tell me, tell me,   49
  How showed his tasking? Seemed it in contempt?   50

VERNON
  No, by my soul. I never in my life
  Did hear a challenge urged more modestly,   52
  Unless a brother should a brother dare
  To gentle exercise and proof of arms.   54
  He gave you all the duties of a man,   55
  Trimmed up your praises with a princely tongue,   56
  Spoke your deservings like a chronicle,
  Making you ever better than his praise
  By still dispraising praise valued with you;   59

---

42 brave proud   **43 engaged** held as hostage   **49 Monmouth** (A name for
the Prince taken from the Welsh town where he was born.)   **50 showed his
tasking** appeared his giving the challenge   **52 urged** put forward
54 proof test   **55 duties** due merits   **56 Trimmed . . . praises** adorned his
praise of you   **59 dispraising** disparaging. **valued** compared

And, which became him like a prince indeed,
He made a blushing cital of himself,   61
And chid his truant youth with such a grace   62
As if he mastered there a double spirit
Of teaching and of learning instantly.   64
There did he pause. But let me tell the world,
If he outlive the envy of this day,   66
England did never owe so sweet a hope,   67
So much misconstrued in his wantonness.   68

HOTSPUR
Cousin, I think thou art enamorèd
On his follies. Never did I hear
Of any prince so wild a liberty.   71
But be he as he will, yet once ere night
I will embrace him with a soldier's arm,
That he shall shrink under my courtesy.   74
Arm, arm with speed! And, fellows, soldiers, friends,
Better consider what you have to do
Than I, that have not well the gift of tongue,
Can lift your blood up with persuasion.

        Enter a Messenger.

FIRST MESSENGER   My lord, here are letters for you.
HOTSPUR   I cannot read them now.
O gentlemen, the time of life is short!
To spend that shortness basely were too long
If life did ride upon a dial's point,   83
Still ending at the arrival of an hour.   84
An if we live, we live to tread on kings;
If die, brave death, when princes die with us!   86
Now, for our consciences, the arms are fair   87
When the intent of bearing them is just.

        Enter another [Messenger].

SECOND MESSENGER
My lord, prepare. The King comes on apace.

61 cital account, citation   **62 chid** chided   **64 instantly** simultaneously
66 envy hostility   **67 owe** own   **68 wantonness** playful sportiveness
71 liberty licentiousness   **74 shrink under my courtesy** (1) be daunted by
my greater courtesy (2) fall back before my attack   **83 If** even if.   **dial's
point** hand of a watch   **84 Still . . . hour** ineluctably concluding within an
hour's time   **86 brave** glorious   **87 for** as for.   **fair** just

HOTSPUR

  I thank him that he cuts me from my tale,
  For I profess not talking. Only this—
  Let each man do his best. And here draw I
  A sword, whose temper I intend to stain
  With the best blood that I can meet withal
  In the adventure of this perilous day.
  Now, *Esperance*! Percy! And set on.   96
  Sound all the lofty instruments of war,
  And by that music let us all embrace;
  For, heaven to earth, some of us never shall   99
  A second time do such a courtesy.

                       Here they embrace. [*Exeunt.*]

5.3   *The trumpets sound. The King enters with his*
        power [*and passes over the stage*]. *Alarum to*
        the battle. Then enter Douglas, and Sir Walter
        Blunt [*dressed like King Henry*].

BLUNT

  What is thy name, that in the battle thus
  Thou crossest me? What honor dost thou seek
  Upon my head?

DOUGLAS   Know then my name is Douglas,
  And I do haunt thee in the battle thus
  Because some tell me that thou art a king.

BLUNT   They tell thee true.

DOUGLAS

  The lord of Stafford dear today hath bought   7
  Thy likeness, for instead of thee, King Harry,   8
  This sword hath ended him. So shall it thee,
  Unless thou yield thee as my prisoner.

BLUNT

  I was not born a yielder, thou proud Scot,
  And thou shalt find a king that will revenge

96 Esperance (The motto of the Percy family.)   **99 heaven to earth** i.e.,
I'll wager heaven against earth

5.3. Location: Shrewsbury field. The scene is virtually continuous.
s.d. power army. **Alarum** trumpet signal to advance **7 dear** dearly
7–8 bought Thy likeness paid for his resemblance to you

Lord Stafford's death. *They fight. Douglas kills Blunt.*

    Then enter Hotspur.

HOTSPUR
  O Douglas, hadst thou fought at Holmedon thus,
  I never had triumphed upon a Scot.
DOUGLAS
  All's done, all's won; here breathless lies the King.   16
HOTSPUR Where?
DOUGLAS Here.
HOTSPUR
  This, Douglas? No. I know this face full well.
  A gallant knight he was; his name was Blunt,
  Semblably furnished like the King himself.   21
DOUGLAS
  A fool go with thy soul, whither it goes!   22
  A borrowed title hast thou bought too dear.
  Why didst thou tell me that thou wert a king?
HOTSPUR
  The King hath many marching in his coats.   25
DOUGLAS
  Now, by my sword, I will kill all his coats!
  I'll murder all his wardrobe, piece by piece,
  Until I meet the King.
HOTSPUR   Up and away!
  Our soldiers stand full fairly for the day.   *[Exeunt.]* 29

    Alarum. Enter Falstaff, solus.

FALSTAFF Though I could scape shot-free at London, I 30
fear the shot here; here's no scoring but upon the pate. 31
Soft, who are you? Sir Walter Blunt. There's honor for
you. Here's no vanity! I am as hot as molten lead, and 33
as heavy too. God keep lead out of me! I need no more

---

16 breathless i.e., dead   **21 Semblably furnished** similarly accoutered
22 A . . . soul i.e., may the stigma of "fool" accompany your soul (for
having dressed as a decoy of King Henry)   **25 coats** vests worn over
armor embroidered with a coat of arms   **29 stand . . . day** i.e., seem in
an auspicious position, likely to win the victory   **30 shot-free** without
paying the tavern bill   **31 scoring** (1) cutting (2) marking up of charges,
by notches on a stick or on the inn door   **33 Here's no vanity** i.e.
(ironically), if this doesn't show what I was saying about honor, then
nothing does

weight than mine own bowels. I have led my raga-
muffins where they are peppered. There's not three of
my hundred and fifty left alive, and they are for the
town's end, to beg during life. But who comes here?   38

    Enter the Prince.

PRINCE
What, stands thou idle here? Lend me thy sword.
Many a nobleman lies stark and stiff
Under the hoofs of vaunting enemies,
Whose deaths are yet unrevenged. I prithee,
Lend me thy sword.
FALSTAFF O Hal, I prithee, give me leave to breathe
awhile. Turk Gregory never did such deeds in arms as   45
I have done this day. I have paid Percy, I have made   46
him sure.   47
PRINCE
He is, indeed, and living to kill thee.
I prithee, lend me thy sword.
FALSTAFF Nay, before God, Hal, if Percy be alive, thou
gets not my sword; but take my pistol, if thou wilt.
PRINCE
Give it me. What, is it in the case?
FALSTAFF Ay, Hal, 'tis hot, 'tis hot. There's that will sack 53
a city.   *The Prince draws it out, and finds it to be a*
                                 bottle of sack.
PRINCE What, is it a time to jest and dally now?
               He throws the bottle at him. Exit.
FALSTAFF Well, if Percy be alive, I'll pierce him. If he do 56
come in my way, so; if he do not, if I come in his   57
willingly, let him make a carbonado of me. I like not   58
such grinning honor as Sir Walter hath. Give me life,

---

38 town's end i.e., city gate, frequented by beggars   **45 Turk Gregory**
(*Turk* is an abusive term signifying a tyrant, and *Gregory* refers probably to Pope Gregory XIII, who was assumed to have encouraged the
Massacre of Saint Bartholomew [1572] in which many French Protes-
tants were slain, and to have encouraged plots against Elizabeth.)
46–47 made him sure made sure of him. (But Hal takes *sure* in a different sense, meaning "safe.")   **53 hot** (Falstaff implies he has been firing
at the enemy.)   **56 Percy . . . pierce** (Elizabethan pronunciation rendered
the pun more obvious than it is now.)   **57 so** well and good
58 carbonado meat scored across for broiling

which if I can save, so; if not, honor comes unlooked
for, and there's an end.   [*Exit.*] 61

5.4   *Alarum. Excursions. Enter the King, the*
            Prince, Lord John of Lancaster, [and the] Earl
            of Westmorland.

KING   I prithee,
  Harry, withdraw thyself; thou bleedest too much.
  Lord John of Lancaster, go you with him.
LANCASTER
  Not I, my lord, unless I did bleed too.
PRINCE
  I beseech Your Majesty make up,   5
  Lest your retirement do amaze your friends.   6
KING
  I will do so. My lord of Westmorland,
  Lead him to his tent.
WESTMORLAND
  Come, my lord, I'll lead you to your tent.
PRINCE
  Lead me, my lord? I do not need your help.
  And God forbid a shallow scratch should drive
  The Prince of Wales from such a field as this,
  Where stained nobility lies trodden on
  And rebels' arms triumph in massacres!
LANCASTER
  We breathe too long. Come, cousin Westmorland,   15
  Our duty this way lies. For God's sake, come.
            [*Exeunt Prince John and Westmorland.*]
PRINCE
  By God, thou hast deceived me, Lancaster!
  I did not think thee lord of such a spirit.

61 there's an end (1) that concludes the subject of my catechism (2) thus
life ends

5.4. Location: Scene continues at Shrewsbury field.
s.d. Excursions sorties. (The fallen body of Blunt may be removed at
some point or may be onstage still at 5.4.77 when Hal kills Hotspur.)
5 make up go forward **6 retirement** retreat. **amaze** alarm **15 breathe**
rest, pause for breath (as also at l. 47)

Before, I loved thee as a brother, John,
But now I do respect thee as my soul.

KING
I saw him hold Lord Percy at the point   21
With lustier maintenance than I did look for   22
Of such an ungrown warrior.

PRINCE
O, this boy lends mettle to us all!   *Exit.* 24

    [*Enter Douglas.*]

DOUGLAS
Another king? They grow like Hydra's heads.   25
I am the Douglas, fatal to all those
That wear those colors on them. What art thou   27
That counterfeit'st the person of a king?

KING
The King himself, who, Douglas, grieves at heart
So many of his shadows thou hast met   30
And not the very King. I have two boys
Seek Percy and thyself about the field;   32
But, seeing thou fall'st on me so luckily,
I will assay thee, and defend thyself.   34

DOUGLAS
I fear thou art another counterfeit;
And yet, in faith, thou bearest thee like a king.
But mine I am sure thou art, whoe'er thou be,
And thus I win thee.
                They fight; the King being in danger,
                        enter Prince of Wales.

PRINCE
Hold up thy head, vile Scot, or thou art like   39
Never to hold it up again! The spirits
Of valiant Shirley, Stafford, Blunt, are in my arms.
It is the Prince of Wales that threatens thee,
Who never promiseth but he means to pay.   43
                 They fight. Douglas flieth.

---

21 at the point at sword's point   **22 lustier maintenance** more vigorous
bearing   **24 mettle** spirit   **25 Hydra's heads** (The heads of the Ler-
naean Hydra grew again as fast as they were cut off.)   **27 colors** i.e., the
colors of the King's insignia   **30 shadows** having form without substance   **32 Seek** who seek   **34 assay** put to the test   **39 like** likely
43 pay (1) settle a debt (2) kill

Cheerly, my lord. How fares Your Grace?
Sir Nicholas Gawsey hath for succor sent,
And so hath Clifton. I'll to Clifton straight.
KING   Stay and breathe awhile.
Thou hast redeemed thy lost opinion,   48
And showed thou mak'st some tender of my life   49
In this fair rescue thou hast brought to me.
PRINCE
O God, they did me too much injury
That ever said I hearkened for your death.   52
If it were so, I might have let alone
The insulting hand of Douglas over you,   54
Which would have been as speedy in your end
As all the poisonous potions in the world,
And saved the treacherous labor of your son.
KING
Make up to Clifton; I'll to Sir Nicholas Gawsey.   58

Exit King.

Enter Hotspur.

HOTSPUR
If I mistake not, thou art Harry Monmouth.
PRINCE
Thou speak'st as if I would deny my name.
HOTSPUR
My name is Harry Percy.
PRINCE   Why then I see
A very valiant rebel of the name.
I am the Prince of Wales; and think not, Percy,
To share with me in glory any more.
Two stars keep not their motion in one sphere,
Nor can one England brook a double reign   66
Of Harry Percy and the Prince of Wales.
HOTSPUR
Nor shall it, Harry, for the hour is come
To end the one of us; and would to God
Thy name in arms were now as great as mine!
PRINCE
I'll make it greater ere I part from thee,

48 **opinion** reputation   49 **mak'st ... of** have some care for
52 **hearkened** listened (as for welcome news)   54 **insulting** exulting
58 **Make up** advance   66 **brook** endure

And all the budding honors on thy crest
I'll crop to make a garland for my head.   73

HOTSPUR
I can no longer brook thy vanities.   *They fight.* 74

   Enter Falstaff.

FALSTAFF   Well said, Hal! To it, Hal! Nay, you shall find 75
no boy's play here, I can tell you.   76

   Enter Douglas. He fighteth with Falstaff, who
   falls down as if he were dead. [Exit Douglas.] The
   Prince killeth Percy.

HOTSPUR
O Harry, thou hast robbed me of my youth!
I better brook the loss of brittle life
Than those proud titles thou hast won of me;
They wound my thoughts worse than thy sword my
   flesh.
But thoughts, the slaves of life, and life, time's fool,   81
And time, that takes survey of all the world,
Must have a stop. O, I could prophesy,
But that the earthy and cold hand of death
Lies on my tongue. No, Percy, thou art dust,
And food for—   [*He dies.*]

PRINCE
For worms, brave Percy. Fare thee well, great heart!
Ill-weaved ambition, how much art thou shrunk!
When that this body did contain a spirit,
A kingdom for it was too small a bound;
But now two paces of the vilest earth
Is room enough. This earth that bears thee dead
Bears not alive so stout a gentleman.   93
If thou wert sensible of courtesy,   94
I should not make so dear a show of zeal;   95
But let my favors hide thy mangled face,   96
And, even in thy behalf, I'll thank myself

73 crop pluck   **74 vanities** empty boasts   **75 Well said** well done
76 s.d. killeth mortally wounds   **81 thoughts . . . fool** i.e., our mental
consciousness, which is dependent on physical existence, and our life
itself, which is subject to time   **93 stout** valiant   **94 sensible of courtesy** i.e., able to hear my praise   **95 dear** handsome, heartfelt.   **zeal**
admiration   **96 favors** plume, scarf, glove, or similar article

For doing these fair rites of tenderness.
                    [*He covers Hotspur's face with a scarf
                                    or other favor.*]
Adieu, and take thy praise with thee to heaven!
Thy ignominy sleep with thee in the grave,
But not remembered in thy epitaph!
                    He spieth Falstaff on the ground.
What, old acquaintance, could not all this flesh
Keep in a little life? Poor Jack, farewell!
I could have better spared a better man.
O, I should have a heavy miss of thee   105
If I were much in love with vanity!   106
Death hath not struck so fat a deer today,
Though many dearer, in this bloody fray.
Emboweled will I see thee by and by.   109
Till then in blood by noble Percy lie.   *Exit.*
                                    Falstaff riseth up.
FALSTAFF Emboweled? If thou embowel me today, I'll
give you leave to powder me and eat me too tomor-   112
row. 'Sblood, 'twas time to counterfeit, or that hot ter- 113
magant Scot had paid me, scot and lot too. Counterfeit? 114
I lie, I am no counterfeit. To die is to be a counterfeit,
for he is but the counterfeit of a man who hath not the
life of a man; but to counterfeit dying, when a man
thereby liveth, is to be no counterfeit but the true and
perfect image of life indeed. The better part of valor is 119
discretion, in the which better part I have saved my
life. Zounds, I am afraid of this gunpowder Percy,
though he be dead. How if he should counterfeit too
and rise? By my faith, I am afraid he would prove the
better counterfeit. Therefore I'll make him sure; yea,
and I'll swear I killed him. Why may not he rise as well
as I? Nothing confutes me but eyes, and nobody sees   126
me. Therefore, sirrah [*Stabbing him*], with a new

---

105 heavy (1) serious (2) corpulent **106 vanity** frivolity **109 Emboweled**
disemboweled, i.e., for embalming and burial **112 powder** salt
113–114 termagant violent and blustering, like the heathen god of the
Saracens in medieval and Renaissance lore **114 paid** i.e., killed. **scot
and lot** i.e., completely. (Originally the phrase was the term for a parish
tax.) **119 part** constituent part, quality, role **126 Nothing . . . eyes** i.e.,
nothing can contradict me but an eyewitness

wound in your thigh, come you along with me.
                    He takes up Hotspur on his back.

Enter Prince [and] John of Lancaster.

PRINCE
Come, brother John; full bravely hast thou fleshed   129
Thy maiden sword.
LANCASTER   But soft, whom have we here?
Did you not tell me this fat man was dead?
PRINCE   I did; I saw him dead,
Breathless and bleeding on the ground.—Art thou alive?
Or is it fantasy that plays upon our eyesight?
I prithee, speak. We will not trust our eyes
Without our ears. Thou art not what thou seem'st.
FALSTAFF   No, that's certain, I am not a double man; but   137
if I be not Jack Falstaff, then am I a Jack. There is Percy   138
[*Throwing the body down*]. If your father will do me
any honor, so; if not, let him kill the next Percy him-
self. I look to be either earl or duke, I can assure you.

PRINCE
Why, Percy I killed myself and saw thee dead.
FALSTAFF   Didst thou? Lord, Lord, how this world is
given to lying! I grant you I was down and out of
breath, and so was he; but we rose both at an instant   145
and fought a long hour by Shrewsbury clock. If I may
be believed, so; if not, let them that should reward
valor bear the sin upon their own heads. I'll take it   148
upon my death, I gave him this wound in the thigh.   149
If the man were alive and would deny it, zounds, I
would make him eat a piece of my sword.
LANCASTER
This is the strangest tale that ever I heard.
PRINCE
This is the strangest fellow, brother John.—
Come, bring your luggage nobly on your back.
For my part, if a lie may do thee grace,   155

129 fleshed initiated (in battle)   **137 double man** (1) specter (2) two
men   **138 Jack** knave   **145 at an instant** simultaneously   **148–149 take
. . . death** i.e., swear with my eternal soul at risk   **155 a lie** i.e., this lie
of yours. **grace** credit

I'll gild it with the happiest terms I have.   156
      A retreat is sounded.
The trumpet sounds retreat; the day is ours.
Come, brother, let us to the highest of the field,   158
To see what friends are living, who are dead.
    Exeunt [Prince of Wales and Lancaster].
FALSTAFF I'll follow, as they say, for reward. He that re-
wards me, God reward him! If I do grow great, I'll
grow less; for I'll purge, and leave sack, and live   162
cleanly as a nobleman should do.
      Exit [bearing off the body].

        ♣

5.5 *The trumpets sound. Enter the King, Prince of*
   Wales, Lord John of Lancaster, Earl of
   Westmorland, with Worcester and Vernon
   prisoners.

KING
 Thus ever did rebellion find rebuke.
 Ill-spirited Worcester! Did not we send grace,
 Pardon, and terms of love to all of you?
 And wouldst thou turn our offers contrary?   4
 Misuse the tenor of thy kinsman's trust?   5
 Three knights upon our party slain today,
 A noble earl, and many a creature else
 Had been alive this hour,
 If like a Christian thou hadst truly borne
 Betwixt our armies true intelligence.   10
WORCESTER
 What I have done my safety urged me to;
 And I embrace this fortune patiently,
 Since not to be avoided it falls on me.

---

156 happiest most felicitous **158 highest** highest vantage point
162 purge (1) reduce in weight, using laxatives (2) repent

5.5. Location: The battlefield.
4 turn . . . contrary reverse the intention of our offers **5 Misuse . . .
trust** i.e., abuse Hotspur's confidence (by concealing the generosity of
my offer, in your role as emissary) **10 intelligence** information, report

KING
   Bear Worcester to the death and Vernon too.
   Other offenders we will pause upon.
              [*Exeunt Worcester and Vernon, guarded.*]
   How goest the field?
PRINCE
   The noble Scot, Lord Douglas, when he saw
   The fortune of the day quite turned from him,
   The noble Percy slain, and all his men
   Upon the foot of fear, fled with the rest;   20
   And falling from a hill, he was so bruised
   That the pursuers took him. At my tent
   The Douglas is; and I beseech Your Grace
   I may dispose of him.
KING   With all my heart.
PRINCE
   Then, brother John of Lancaster,
   To you this honorable bounty shall belong.   26
   Go to the Douglas and deliver him
   Up to his pleasure, ransomless and free.
   His valors shown upon our crests today   29
   Have taught us how to cherish such high deeds
   Even in the bosom of our adversaries.
LANCASTER
   I thank Your Grace for this high courtesy,
   Which I shall give away immediately.   33
KING
   Then this remains, that we divide our power.
   You, son John, and my cousin Westmorland
   Towards York shall bend you with your dearest speed 36
   To meet Northumberland and the prelate Scroop,
   Who, as we hear, are busily in arms.
   Myself and you, son Harry, will towards Wales,
   To fight with Glendower and the Earl of March.
   Rebellion in this land shall lose his sway,   41
   Meeting the check of such another day;
   And since this business so fair is done,   43
   Let us not leave till all our own be won.   *Exeunt.* 44

---

20 Upon . . . fear fleeing in panic **26 bounty** assignment, act of benevolence **29 crests** i.e., helmets **33 give away** pass along, confer on Douglas **36 bend you** direct your course. **dearest** most urgent **41 his** its **43 fair** successfully **44 leave** leave off

Date and Text

On February 25, 1598, "The historye of Henry the IIIJ^th with his battaile of Shrewsburye against Henry Hottspurre of the Northe with the conceipted mirthe of Sir John Ffalstoff" was entered in the Stationers' Register, the official record book of the London Company of Stationers (booksellers and printers), by Andrew Wise. Later that year appeared the following quarto:

THE HISTORY OF HENRIE THE FOVRTH; With the battell at Shrewsburie, *betweene the King and Lord* Henry Percy, surnamed Henrie Hotspur of the North. *With the humorous conceits of Sir* Iohn Falstalffe. AT LONDON, Printed by *P. S.* [Peter Short] for *Andrew Wise*, dwelling in Paules Churchyard, at the signe of the Angell. 1598.

Actually this was not the first quarto, for an earlier fragment of eight pages has survived, part of a text that served as copy for the first complete extant quarto. Together these quartos make up an excellent authoritative text, based seemingly on the author's papers or, more probably, a scribal transcript of them. Four more quartos appeared before the First Folio of 1623, each based on the previous quarto. The Folio itself was based on the last of these, perhaps with reference also to some kind of manuscript, although the number of authoritative readings that can be claimed for the Folio is small.

1 Henry IV shows signs of revision in the use of characters' names, most notably that of Falstaff. Plainly the original version of the play called him Sir John Oldcastle, after one of the prince's companions in the anonymous *Famous Victories of Henry the Fifth* (c. 1588). The name "Oldcastle" was originally intended for *2 Henry IV* as well. The speech prefix "Old." is left standing at 1.2.138 in the quarto of *2 Henry IV*, one or two lines of verse in *1 Henry IV* are one syllable short evidently because "Oldcastle" has been altered to "Falstaff," and Falstaff is jokingly referred to as "my old lad of the castle" (*1 Henry IV*, 1.2.41). Moreover, there are several contemporary allusions to a play about a fat knight named Oldcastle. Apparently Henry Brooke,

Lord Cobham, a living descendant of the Lollard martyr Oldcastle of Henry V's reign, took umbrage at the profane use Shakespeare had made of this revered name, whereupon Shakespeare's acting company shifted to another less controversial name from the chronicles, Sir John Fastolfe or Falstaff (called "Falstaffe" in the Folio text of Shakespeare's *1 Henry VI* and assigned a cowardly role in the French wars of that play). The revision also changed the names of Oldcastle's cronies from Harvey and Russell to Peto and Bardolph. This edition retains the name "Falstaff" since Shakespeare clearly accepted it as the new name of the character in all his "Falstaff" plays.

Cobham was Lord Chamberlain from July 1596 until his death in March 1597, during which interval Shakespeare's company bore the name of Lord Hunsdon's men. Quite possibly the difficulty over the name Oldcastle erupted during that period, for *1 Henry IV* seems to have been written and performed in late 1596 and early 1597 not long after Shakespeare had finished *Richard II* (c. 1595–1596).

Francis Meres, in his *Palladis Tamia: Wit's Treasury* (a slender volume on contemporary literature and art; valuable because it lists most of the plays of Shakespeare's that existed at that time), refers in 1598 to "*Henry the* 4" without specifying one or two parts. Publication of *1 Henry IV* in 1598 confirmed to the Elizabethan public that the changes in names to Falstaff, Peto, and Bardolph had taken place.

Textual Notes

These textual notes are not a historical collation, either of the early quartos and the early folios or of more recent editions; they are simply a record of departures in this edition from the copy text. The reading adopted in this edition appears in boldface, followed by the rejected reading from the copy text, i.e., the first quarto of 1598. Only major alterations in punctuation are noted. Changes in lineation are not indicated, nor are some minor and obvious typographical errors.

Abbreviations used:
F the First Folio
Q quarto
s.d. stage direction
s.p. speech prefix

Copy text: the first complete quarto of 1598 [Q1]; and, for 1.3.201 through 2.2.110, the fragment of an earlier quarto (Q0).

1.1. 22 levy leauy   **39 Herefordshire** Herdforshire   **62 a dear** deere   **76 In faith, it is** [assigned in Q1 to King]

1.2. 16 king a king   **78 similes** smiles   **154 thou** the   **158 Peto, Bardolph** Haruey, Rossill

1.3. 194 good night god-night   **201 s.p. Hotspur** [missing in Q0–Q4]   **238 whipped** [Q1] whip [Q0]

2.1. 34 s.p. First Carrier Car   **48 s.d.** [at l. 47 in Q0]

2.2. s.d. Poins, Peto Poines, and Peto &c   **20 Bardolph** Bardol [and thus, or "Bardoll," throughout the play]   **34 mine** [Q1] my [Q0]   **42 Go hang** [F] Hang [Q0]   **51 s.p. and text BARDOLPH** What news [all assigned as continuation of Poins's speech in l. 50]   **52 s.p. Gadshill** Bar   **78 s.p. First Traveler** Trauel   **82 s.p. Travelers** Trauel   **86 s.p. Travelers** Tra

2.3. 1 s.p. Hotspur [not in Q1]   **4 In** In the   **48 thee** the

2.4. 33 precedent present   **36 s.p. Poins** Prin   **171 s.p. Prince** Gad   **172 s.p. Gadshill** Ross [also at ll. 174 and 178]   **226 keech** catch   **242 eelskin** ellskin   **322 s.d.** [at l. 321 in Q1]   **337 Owen** O   **390 tristful** trustfull   **398 yet so** yet   **468 lean** lane   **518 Good** God [also at l. 519]   **526 s.d. pockets** pocket   **530 s.p. Peto** [not in Q1]   **535 s.p. Prince** [not in Q1]

3.1. 97 cantle scantle   **126 meter** miter

3.2. 84 gorged gordge   **145 northern** Northren   **161 s.d.** [at. l. 162 in Q1]

3.3. 35 that's that   **57 tithe** tight   **173 guests** ghesse   **200 o' clock** of clocke

4.1. 1 s.p. [and elsewhere] Hotspur Per   **20 lord** mind   **55 is** tis   **108 dropped** drop   **116 altar** altars   **123 ne'er** neare   **126 cannot** can   **127 yet** it

4.2. 3 Coldfield cophill   **15 yeomen's** Yeomans   **31 feazed** fazd   **81 s.d. Exit** Exeunt

4.3. 23 horse horses **74 heirs . . . followed** heires, as Pages followed
84 country's Countrey

4.4. 18 o'erruled ouerrulde

5.1. s.d. Lancaster Lancaster, Earle of Westmerland **3 southern** Southren
88 off of **114 s.d. Exeunt** Exit **138 will it** will

5.2. 3 undone vnder one **8 Suspicion** Supposition **12 merrily** merely
25 s.d. Hotspur Percy **79 s.p. First Messenger** Mes **89 s.p. Second Messenger** Mes

5.3. 22 A Ah

5.4. 4 s.p. [and elsewhere] Lancaster P. Iohn **68 Nor** Now **76 s.d. who** he
92 thee the

Shakespeare's Sources

Shakespeare's chief historical source for *1 Henry IV* was the 1587 edition of Raphael Holinshed's *Chronicles,* but he also took some important ideas from Samuel Daniel's *The First Four Books of the Civil Wars* (1595). Relevant passages from both sources appear in the following pages. Following Daniel, Shakespeare readjusts the age of Hotspur (who was historically older than Henry IV) to match that of Prince Hal. Daniel's Hotspur is, like Shakespeare's, dauntless and stubborn, a turbulent yet noble spirit. The theme of a nemesis of rebellion afflicting Henry IV for his usurpation, only touched upon in Shakespeare's play, owes something to Daniel's presentation, although the idea of nemesis is to be found also in Holinshed. Both Holinshed and Daniel err in confusing the Edmund Mortimer whom Glendower captured with his nephew Edmund Mortimer, claimant to the throne; Shakespeare perpetuates this error. Hal's killing of Hotspur is unhistorical, since both Holinshed and Daniel report only that Hal bravely helped rescue his father from attack and that Hotspur was killed in the melee. Daniel does give prominence to Prince Henry in the battle, however, and implies that he and Hotspur will meet face-to-face. Shakespeare invents the scenes in which we see Mortimer as a devoted husband and Hotspur as a fond combatant in wit with his wife, Kate; Holinshed merely informs us that both these men were married. Shakespeare greatly expands Glendower's fascination with magic and poetry, changing him from a ruthless barbarian (in Holinshed) into a cranky but charismatic Welshman. Hotspur, despite hints from Daniel and Holinshed, is chiefly Shakespeare's creation.

The most impressive transformations are those of Hal and Falstaff. Shakespeare knew many legends of Hal's wild youth, some from John Stow's *The Chronicles of England* (1580) and *The Annals of England* (1592), others from oral tradition. Many of these stories were also available in Holinshed. Shakespeare's readiest source, however, was a rowdy and chauvinistic play called *The Famous Victories of Henry the Fifth,* registered 1594 but usually ascribed to

Richard Tarleton or Samuel Rowley around 1587 or 1588. A brief selection follows. This play covers all the events of the *Henry IV* plays and *Henry V* in one chaotic sequence. Prince Hal has three companions, Sir John Oldcastle, Tom, and Ned (cf. Ned Poins), in whose company he robs the King's receivers of £1,000, visits the old tavern in Eastcheap, vexes his father, and strikes the Lord Chief Justice. A crucial difference is that this Hal is truly unregenerate. He not only chases after women and robs, but encourages his companions to look forward to unrestricted license when he is King. Hal seems consciously to desire his father's death. Yet he does reform, and banishes his companions beyond a ten-mile limit with a promise to assist them if they amend their conduct. Although Hal's reform is crude and sudden, his popularity aids him when he goes to war against the French. He is followed by a comic crew of London artisans and thieves, who prove invincible against the effete enemy.

Shakespeare owes much to this unsophisticated, vibrant account of Hal's riotous youth, but he has transformed it to his own use. He limits himself in *1 Henry IV* to the action leading up to the Battle of Shrewsbury in order to focus on the coming of age of Prince Henry and the pairing and contrasting of Hotspur, Falstaff, and King Henry IV as alternative models for Hal's behavior. He invents unforgettable comic characters such as Mistress Quickly, Francis, and Bardolph. Most of all, Shakespeare's portrayal of Falstaff is essentially his own. Sir John Oldcastle of the anonymous play is a minor character, not Hal's closest companion. Falstaff owes something to the tradition of the guileful and inventive Vice of the Tudor morality play (especially when Falstaff is called jestingly "that reverend Vice, that gray Iniquity"; 2.4.448), but the influence of the morality play is general rather than specific. To label Falstaff a "Vice" is to reduce him to comic tempter and villain. Falstaff is in part an allowed fool, a parasite, and a *miles gloriosus* or braggart soldier, but he transcends all these conventionalized types with his own unique vitality.

1 Henry IV suggests some acquaintance with the anonymous play *Thomas of Woodstock* (c. 1591–1595), which Shakespeare may also have used in *Richard II*, and with the complaints of Owen Glendower and Northumberland in *A Mirror for Magistrates* (1559). In neither case is the debt extensive. More suggestive as possible sources are events and social conditions in Shakespeare's England: the Northern Rebellion of 1569 against Queen Elizabeth's government, abuses of military authority by unscrupulous officers, the dangerous state of the highways, the raucous vitality of tavern life in Eastcheap, and the like.

The Third Volume of Chronicles (1587 edition)
Compiled by Raphael Holinshed

HENRY THE FOURTH

[From the beginning of his reign, King Henry IV encounters opposition, especially in the north and along the Welsh border. Henry leads an expedition against Scotland in 1402.]

In the King's absence, whilst he was forth of the realm in Scotland against his enemies, the Welshmen took occasion to rebel under the conduct of their captain Owen Glendower, doing what mischief they could devise unto their English neighbors. This Owen Glendower was son to an esquire of Wales named Griffith Vichan. He dwelled in the parish of Conway, within the county of Merioneth in North Wales, in a place called Glindourwie, which is as much to say in English as "the valley by the side of the water of Dee"; by occasion whereof he was surnamed Glindour Dew.

He was first set to study the laws of the realm, and became an utter barrister[1] or an apprentice of the law (as they term him) and served King Richard at Flint Castle when he was taken by Henry, Duke of Lancaster, though other have written that he served this King Henry the Fourth, before he came to attain the crown, in room[2] of an esquire.

[One sign of civil unrest is an attempt made on the life of King Henry IV, from which he manages to escape unharmed.]

---

1 **utter barrister** one called to the bar and having the privilege of practicing as advocate; utter barristers sit uttermost or outermost on the forms that are called the bar, this being the most senior place in the house next to the benchers   2 **room** position

Howbeit, he was not so soon delivered from fear, for he might well have his life in suspicion and provide for the preservation of the same, sith[3] perils of death crept into his secret chamber and lay lurking in the bed of down where his body was to be reposed and to take rest. O, what a suspected[4] state therefore is that of a king holding his regiment[5] with the hatred of his people, the heartgrudgings of his courtiers, and the peremptory practices[6] of both together! Could he confidently compose or settle himself to sleep for fear of strangling? Durst he boldly eat and drink without dread of poisoning? Might he adventure to show himself in great meetings or solemn[7] assemblies without mistrust of mischief against his person intended? What pleasure or what felicity could he take in his princely pomp, which he knew by manifest and fearful experience to be envied and maligned to the very death?

[Other prodigies attest to the unquiet times of Henry IV.]

Owen Glendower, according to his accustomed manner robbing and spoiling[8] within the English borders, caused all the forces of the shire of Hereford to assemble together against them under the conduct of Edmund Mortimer, Earl of March. But coming to try the matter by battle, whether by treason or otherwise, so it fortuned that the English power was discomfited,[9] the Earl taken prisoner, and above a thousand of his people slain in the place. The shameful villainy used by the Welshwomen towards the dead carcasses was such as honest ears would be ashamed to hear and continent[10] tongues to speak thereof. The dead bodies might not be buried without great sums of money given for liberty[11] to convey them away.

The King was not hasty to purchase the deliverance of the Earl of March, because his title to the crown was well enough known, and therefore suffered him to remain in miserable prison, wishing both the said Earl and all other of his lineage out of this life with God and his saints in

3 **sith** since   4 **suspected** regarded with suspicion   5 **holding his regiment** ruling   6 **heartgrudgings . . . peremptory practices** heartfelt discontent . . . obstinate conspirings   7 **solemn** ceremonial   8 **spoiling** plundering   9 **discomfited** routed, defeated   10 **continent** temperate   11 **liberty** permission

heaven so they had been out of the way,[12] for then all had been well enough as he thought. But to let these things pass, the King this year sent his eldest daughter, Blanche, accompanied with the Earl of Somerset, the Bishop of Worcester, the Lord Clifford, and others, into Almaine,[13] which brought her to Cologne, and there with great triumph she was married to William, Duke of Bavaria, son and heir to Lewis, the Emperor. About mid of August, the King, to chastise the presumptuous attempts of the Welshmen, went with a great power of men into Wales to pursue the Captain of the Welsh rebel, Owen Glendower, but in effect he lost his labor; for Owen conveyed himself out of the way into his known lurking places, and (as was thought) through art magic he caused such foul weather of winds, tempest, rain, snow, and hail to be raised for the annoyance of the King's army that the like had not been heard of; in such sort that the King was constrained to return home, having caused his people yet to spoil and burn first a great part of the country. The same time, the Lord Edmund of Langley, Duke of York, departed this life and was buried at Langley with his brethren. The Scots, under the leading of Patrick Hepborne of the Hales the younger, entering into England were overthrown at Nesbit in the marches,[14] as in the Scottish chronicle ye may find more at large. This battle was fought the two-and-twentieth of June, in this year of our Lord, 1402.

Archibald, Earl Douglas, sore displeased in his mind for this overthrow, procured a commission to invade England, and that to his cost, as ye may likewise read in the Scottish histories. For at a place called Homeldon they were so fiercely assailed by the Englishmen, under the leading of the Lord Percy, surnamed Henry Hotspur, and George, Earl of March, that with violence of the English shot they were quite vanquished and put to flight on the Rood Day[15] in harvest, with a great slaughter made by the Englishmen. . . .

---

12 so . . . way i.e., so long as they were no longer a source of trouble to King Henry. (Holinshed confuses two Mortimers: [1] Sir Edmund Mortimer, son-in-law of Glendower and Hotspur's brother-in-law, and [2] Sir Edmund's nephew, also named Edmund, the fifth Earl of March, who was proclaimed heir to the throne by Richard II in 1398 but who was never captured by Glendower. Shakespeare follows Holinshed's error.) **13 Almaine** Germany **14 marches** frontiers, borders **15 the Rood Day** Holy Rood Day, September 14. (See *1 Henry IV*, 1.1.52.)

There were slain of men of estimation[16] Sir John Swinton, Sir Adam Gordon, Sir John Leviston, Sir Alexander Ramsey of Dalhousie, and three-and-twenty knights, besides ten thousand of the commons; and of prisoners among other were these: Mordake, Earl of Fife, son to the Governor; Archibald, Earl Douglas,[17] which in the fight lost one of his eyes; Thomas, Earl of Murray; Robert, Earl of Angus; and, as some writers have, the Earls of Atholl and Menteith, with five hundred other of meaner degrees.[18] . . .

Edmund Mortimer, Earl of March, prisoner with Owen Glendower, whether for irksomeness of cruel captivity or fear of death or for what other cause it is uncertain, agreed to take part with Owen against the King of England and took to wife the daughter of the said Owen.

Strange wonders happened, as men reported, at the nativity of this man,[19] for the same night he was born, all his father's horses in the stable were found to stand in blood up to the bellies.

[The Percy clan, although they supported Henry in his rebellion against Richard II in 1399, grow increasingly restive during the latter months of 1402.]

Henry, Earl of Northumberland, with his brother Thomas, Earl of Worcester, and his son, the Lord Henry Percy, surnamed Hotspur, which were to King Henry in the beginning of his reign both faithful friends and earnest aiders, began now to envy his wealth and felicity; and especially they were grieved because the King demanded of the Earl and his son such Scottish prisoners as were taken at Homeldon and Nesbit. For of all the captives which were taken in the conflicts foughten in those two places, there was delivered to the King's possession only Mordake, Earl of Fife, the Duke of Albany's son, though the King did

---

16 estimation noble and gentle rank   **17 Mordake . . . Douglas** (In Holinshed, this reads with an error in punctuation: "Mordacke earle of Fife, son to the gouernour archembald earle Dowglas," from which Shakespeare erroneously gathered that Mordake was the son of Archibald; see *1 Henry IV*, 1.1.71–72.)   **18 meaner degrees** lower station **19 this man** (Grammatically this seems to refer to Glendower, and so Shakespeare appears to have understood it at 3.1.12 ff., but Holinshed probably is talking here about the birth of Mortimer.)

divers and sundry times require deliverance of the residue, and that with great threatening. Wherewith the Percys, being sore offended, for that they claimed them as their own proper prisoners and their peculiar prize,[20] by the counsel of the Lord Thomas Percy, Earl of Worcester, whose study was ever, as some write, to procure malice and set things in a broil, came to the King unto Windsor upon a purpose to prove[21] him and there required[22] of him that, either by ransom or otherwise, he would cause to be delivered out of prison Edmund Mortimer, Earl of March, their cousin-german,[23] whom, as they reported, Owen Glendower kept in filthy prison, shackled with irons, only for that he took his part[24] and was to him faithful and true.

The King began not a little to muse at this request, and not without cause; for indeed it touched him somewhat near, sith this Edmund was son to Roger, Earl of March, son to the Lady Philip, daughter of Lionel, Duke of Clarence, the third son of King Edward the Third; which Edmund,[25] at King Richard's going into Ireland, was proclaimed heir apparent to the crown and realm; whose aunt called Eleanor[26] the Lord Henry Percy had married; and therefore King Henry could not well hear that any man should be earnest about the advancement of that lineage. The King, when he had studied on the matter, made answer that the Earl of March was not taken prisoner for his cause nor in his service[27] but willingly suffered himself to be taken, because he would not withstand the attempts of Owen Glendower and his complices,[28] and therefore he would neither ransom him nor relieve him.

The Percys with this answer and fraudulent excuse were not a little fumed,[29] insomuch that Henry Hotspur said openly: "Behold, the heir of the realm is robbed of his right,

---

20 prize booty **21 prove** test **22 required** requested **23 cousin-german** first cousin **24 only for that he took his part** i.e., the Percys requested Henry to ransom the Earl of March because Mortimer was loyal to Henry **25 which Edmund** (In fact, the Earl first named as heir to the Crown was the fourth Earl of March, Roger Mortimer, though his son Edmund was later designated heir when the fourth Earl died.) **26 Eleanor** (Actually, the sister of Sir Edmund Mortimer and of the fourth Earl of March was named Elizabeth. Shakespeare calls her Kate.) **27 his cause . . . his service** i.e., King Henry's cause and service **28 complices** accomplices **29 fumed** incensed

and yet the robber with his own will not redeem him." So in
this fury the Percys departed, minding[30] nothing more than
to depose King Henry from the high type[31] of his royalty and
to place in his seat their cousin Edmund, Earl of March,
whom they did not only deliver out of captivity but also, to
the high displeasure of King Henry, entered in league with
the foresaid Owen Glendower. Herewith they, by their deputies in the house of the Archdeacon of Bangor, divided the
realm amongst them, causing a tripartite indenture to be
made and sealed with their seals, by the covenants whereof
all England from Severn and Trent south and eastward was
assigned to the Earl of March, all Wales and the lands beyond Severn westward were appointed to Owen Glendower,
and all the remnant from Trent northward to the Lord
Percy.

This was done, as some have said, through a foolish credit
given to a vain prophecy, as though King Henry was the
moldwarp,[32] cursed of God's own mouth, and they three
were the dragon, the lion, and the wolf which should divide
this realm between them. Such is the deviation (saith Hall)[33]
and not divination of those blind and fantastical dreams of
the Welsh prophesiers. King Henry, not knowing of this
new confederacy, and nothing less minding than that which
after happened,[34] gathered a great army to go again into
Wales, whereof the Earl of Northumberland and his son
were advertised[35] by the Earl of Worcester, and with all diligence raised all the power they could make and sent to the
Scots which before were taken prisoners at Homeldon for
aid of men, promising to the Earl of Douglas the town of
Berwick and a part of Northumberland and to other Scottish lords great lordships and seigniories if they obtained
the upper hand. The Scots, in hope of gain and desirous to
be revenged of their old griefs,[36] came to the Earl with a
great company well appointed.[37]

The Percys, to make their part seem good, devised certain
articles by the advice of Richard Scroop, Archbishop of

30 **minding** intending   31 **type** summit   32 **moldwarp** mole   33 **Hall**
Edward Hall, author of *The Union of the Two Noble and Illustre Fami-
lies of Lancaster and York* (1542)   34 **nothing . . . happened** not at all
anticipating what eventually took place   35 **advertised** advised, informed   36 **griefs** complaints   37 **appointed** equipped

York, brother to the Lord Scroop, whom King Henry had caused to be beheaded at Bristol. These articles, being showed to divers noblemen and other states[38] of the realm, moved them to favor their purpose, insomuch that many of them did not only promise to the Percys aid and succor by words but also by their writings and seals confirmed the same. Howbeit, when the matter came to trial, the most part of the confederates abandoned them and at the day of the conflict left them alone. Thus, after that the conspirators had discovered themselves,[39] the Lord Henry Percy, desirous to proceed in the enterprise, upon trust to be assisted by Owen Glendower, the Earl of March, and other, assembled an army of men-of-arms and archers forth of Cheshire and Wales. Incontinently[40] his uncle Thomas Percy, Earl of Worcester, that had the government[41] of the Prince of Wales, who as then lay[42] at London in secret manner, conveyed himself out of the Prince's house, and coming to Stafford, where he met his nephew, they increased their power by all ways and means they could devise. The Earl of Northumberland himself was not with them but, being sick, had promised upon his amendment to repair unto them, as some write, with all convenient speed.

These noblemen, to make their conspiracy to seem excusable, besides the articles above-mentioned sent letters abroad,[43] wherein was contained that their gathering of an army tended to none other end but only for the safeguard of their own persons and to put some better government in the commonwealth. For whereas taxes and tallages[44] were daily levied under pretense to be employed in defense of the realm, the same were vainly wasted and unprofitably consumed; and where through the slanderous reports of their enemies the King had taken a grievous displeasure with them, they durst not appear personally in the King's presence until the prelates and barons of the realm had obtained of the King license for them to come and purge themselves before him by lawful trial of their peers, whose judgment, as they pretended, they would in no wise refuse.

38 states noblemen **39 after that . . . themselves** after the conspirators had revealed their purposes **40 Incontinently** immediately **41 government** guardianship **42 lay** resided **43 abroad** round about
44 tallages arbitrary taxes

Many that saw and heard these letters did commend their diligence and highly praised their assured fidelity and trustiness towards the commonwealth. . . .

And to speak a truth, no marvel it was if many envied the prosperous state of King Henry, sith it was evident enough to the world that he had with wrong usurped the crown, and not only violently deposed King Richard but also cruelly procured his death, for the which undoubtedly both he and his posterity tasted such troubles as put them still in danger of their states, till their direct succeeding line was quite rooted out by the contrary faction, as in Henry the Sixth and Edward the Fourth it may appear.

But now to return where we left. King Henry, advertised of the proceedings of the Percys, forthwith gathered about him such power as he might make, and being earnestly called upon by the Scot, the Earl of March,[45] to make haste and give battle to his enemies before their power by delaying of time should still too much increase, he passed forward with such speed that he was in sight of his enemies, lying in camp near to Shrewsbury, before they were in doubt of[46] any such thing; for the Percys thought that he would have stayed at Burton-upon-Trent till his council had come thither to him to give their advice what he were best to do. But herein the enemy was deceived of his expectation, sith the King had great regard of expedition and making speed for the safety of his own person whereunto the Earl of March incited him, considering that in delay is danger and loss in lingering, as the poet in the like case saith:

> Dum trepidant nullo firmatae robore partes,
> Tolle moras; semper nocuit differre paratis.[47]

By reason of the King's sudden coming in this sort, they stayed[48] from assaulting the town of Shrewsbury, which enterprise they were ready at that instant to have taken in hand; and forthwith the Lord Percy, as a captain of high

---

45 Scot . . . March i.e., George Dunbar, Earl of March of Scotland, not to be confused with Edmund Mortimer, the Earl of March in England **46 were in doubt of** feared, anticipated **47 Dum . . . partes** (An often-quoted maxim from Lucan's *Pharsalia*, 1:280–281, to the effect that it is folly to allow one's enemies to consolidate power, and that delay is always harmful once you are prepared. Holinshed prints the lines in reverse order.) **48 stayed** refrained, withheld

courage, began to exhort the captains and soldiers to prepare themselves to battle, sith the matter was grown to that
point that by no means it could be avoided. "So that," said
he, "this day shall either bring us all to advancement and
honor, or else, if it shall chance us to be overcome, shall
deliver us from the King's spiteful malice and cruel dis-
dain; for playing the men, as we ought to do, better it is to
die in battle for the commonwealth's cause than through
cowardlike fear to prolong life which after shall be taken
from us by sentence of the enemy."

Hereupon the whole army, being in number about fourteen thousand chosen men, promised to stand with him so
long as life lasted. There were with the Percys as chieftains
of this army the Earl of Douglas, a Scottish man; the Baron
of Kinderton; Sir Hugh Browne and Sir Richard Vernon,
knights; with divers other stout and right valiant captains.
Now when the two armies were encamped, the one against
the other, the Earl of Worcester and the Lord Percy with
their complices sent the articles (whereof I spake before)
by Thomas Caton and Thomas Salvain, esquires, to King
Henry, under their hands and seals, which articles in effect
charged him with manifest perjury, in that, contrary to his
oath received upon the evangelists at Doncaster when he
first entered the realm after his exile, he had taken upon
him the crown and royal dignity, imprisoned King Richard,
caused him to resign his title and finally to be murdered.
Divers other matters they laid to his charge, as levying
of taxes and tallages contrary to his promise, infringing of
laws and customs of the realm, and suffering the Earl of
March to remain in prison without travailing[49] to have him
delivered. All which things they, as procurers and protec-
tors of the commonwealth, took upon them to prove against
him, as they protested unto the whole world.

King Henry, after he had read their articles, with the defiance which they annexed to the same, answered the esquires that he was ready with dint of sword and fierce
battle to prove their quarrel false and nothing else than a
forged matter, not doubting but that God would aid and assist him in his righteous cause against the disloyal and false

49 travailing laboring

forsworn traitors. The next day in the morning early, being the even of Mary Magdalene,[50] they set their battles[51] in order on both sides, and now, whilst the warriors looked when the token of battle should be given, the Abbot of Shrewsbury and one of the clerks of the Privy Seal were sent from the King unto the Percys to offer them pardon if they would come to any reasonable agreement. By their persuasions, the Lord Henry Percy began to give ear unto the King's offer and so sent with them his uncle, the Earl of Worcester, to declare unto the King the causes of those troubles and to require some effectual reformation in the same.

It was reported for a truth that now, when the King had condescended unto all that was reasonable at his hands to be required and seemed to humble himself more than was meet for his estate, the Earl of Worcester, upon his return to his nephew, made relation clean contrary to that[52] the King had said in such sort that he set his nephew's heart more in displeasure towards the King than ever it was before, driving him by that means to fight whether he would or not. Then suddenly blew the trumpets, the King's part[53] crying "Saint George! Upon them!" The adversaries cried "Esperance! Percy!" and so the two armies furiously joined. The archers on both sides shot for the best game, laying on such load with arrows that many died and were driven down that never rose again.

The Scots, as some write, which had the foreward[54] on the Percys' side, intending to be revenged of their old displeasures done to them by the English nation, set so fiercely on the King's foreward, led by the Earl of Stafford, that they made the same draw back and had almost broken their adversaries' array. The Welshmen also, which before had lain lurking in the woods, mountains, and marshes, hearing of this battle toward,[55] came to the aid of the Percys and refreshed the wearied people with new succors. The King, perceiving that his men were thus put to distress what with the violent impression[56] of the Scots and the tempestuous

---

50 the even of Mary Magdalene the eve before the Feast of Mary Magdalene on July 22 (1403)   **51 battles** battalions, armed forces   **52 that** that which   **53 part** supporters   **54 foreward** vanguard   **55 toward** impending, at hand   **56 impression** assault, attack

storms of arrows that his adversaries discharged freely against him and his people, it was no need to will him to stir; for suddenly, with his fresh battle,[57] he approached and relieved his men, so that the battle began more fierce than before. Here the Lord Henry Percy and the Earl Douglas, a right stout and hardy captain, not regarding the shot of the King's battle nor the close order of the ranks, pressing forward together bent their whole forces towards the King's person, coming upon him with spears and swords so fiercely that the Earl of March the Scot, perceiving their purpose, withdrew the King from that side of the field, as some write, for his great benefit and safeguard, as it appeared. For they gave such a violent onset upon them that stood about the King's standard that, slaying his standard-bearer, Sir Walter Blunt, and overthrowing the standard, they made slaughter of all those that stood about it, as[58] the Earl of Stafford, that day made by the King Constable of the realm, and divers other.

The Prince that day holp his father like a lusty young gentleman; for although he was hurt in the face with an arrow, so that divers noblemen that were about him would have conveyed him forth of the field, yet he would not suffer them so to do, lest his departure from amongst his men might haply have stricken some fear into their hearts. And so, without regard of his hurt, he continued with his men and never ceased either to fight where the battle was most hot or to encourage his men where it seemed most need. This battle lasted three long hours with indifferent fortune on both parts till at length the King, crying "Saint George! Victory!" brake the array of his enemies and adventured so far that, as some write, the Earl Douglas strake him down and at that instant slew Sir Walter Blunt and three other appareled in the King's suit and clothing, saying: "I marvel to see so many kings thus suddenly arise one in the neck of[59] another." The King indeed was raised and did that day many a noble feat of arms, for as it is written, he slew that day with his own hands six-and-thirty persons of his enemies. The other on his part,[60] encouraged by his doings,

57 battle battalion   58 as such as, including   59 in the neck of immediately following   60 The other on his part others in his army. (Not, as it might be interpreted, a reference to Prince Henry.)

fought valiantly and slew the Lord Percy, called Sir Henry Hotspur. To conclude, the King's enemies were vanquished and put to flight, in which flight the Earl of Douglas, for haste, falling from the crag of an high mountain, brake one of his cullions[61] and was taken, and, for his valiantness, of the King frankly[62] and freely delivered.

There was also taken the Earl of Worcester, the procurer and setter-forth of all this mischief, Sir Richard Vernon, and the Baron of Kinderton, with divers other. There were slain upon the King's part, besides the Earl of Stafford, to the number of ten knights: Sir Hugh Shirley, Sir John Clifton, Sir John Cokayne, Sir Nicholas Gawsey, Sir Walter Blunt, Sir John Calverley, Sir John Massey of Podington, Sir Hugh Mortimer, and Sir Robert Gawsey, all the which received the same morning the order of knighthood; Sir Thomas Wensley was wounded to death and so passed out of this life shortly after. There died in all upon the King's side sixteen hundred, and four thousand were grievously wounded. On the contrary side were slain, besides the Lord Percy, the most part of the knights and esquires of the county of Chester, to the number of two hundred, besides yeomen and footmen; in all there died of those that fought on the Percys' side about five thousand. This battle was fought on Mary Magdalene Even, being Saturday. Upon the Monday following, the Earl of Worcester, the Baron of Kinderton, and Sir Richard Vernon, knights, were condemned and beheaded. The Earl's head was sent to London, there to be set on the Bridge.

[Holinshed gives an account of friction between King Henry and his son, although from a considerably later date, 1412, and having no connection with the Percy rebellion and the Battle of Shrewsbury.]

The Lord Henry, Prince of Wales, eldest son to King Henry, got knowledge that certain of his father's servants were busy to give informations against him, whereby discord might arise betwixt him and his father; for they put into the King's head not only what evil rule (according to the course of youth) the Prince kept, to the offense of many,

61 cullions testicles **62 frankly** generously

but also what great resort of people came to his house, so
that the court was nothing[63] furnished with such a train as
daily followed the Prince. These tales brought no small suspicion into the King's head, lest his son would presume to
usurp the Crown, he being yet alive, through which suspicious jealousy it was perceived that he favored not his son
as in times past he had done.

The Prince, sore offended with such persons as, by slanderous reports, sought not only to spot his good name
abroad in the realm but to sow discord also betwixt him
and his father, wrote his letters into every part of the
realm to reprove[64] all such slanderous devices of those that
sought his discredit. And to clear himself the better, that
the world might understand what wrong he had to be slandered in such wise, about the feast of Peter and Paul, to wit
the nine-and-twentieth day of June, he came to the court
with such a number of noblemen and other his friends that
wished him well as the like train had been seldom seen re-
pairing to the court at any one time in those days. He was
appareled in a gown of blue satin full of small eyelet holes,
at every hole the needle hanging by a silk thread with which
it was sewed. About his arm he ware an hound's collar set
full of SS of gold and the terrets[65] likewise being of the
same metal.

The court was then at Westminster where, he being entered into the hall, not one of his company durst once advance himself further than the fire in the same hall,
notwithstanding they were earnestly requested by the lords
to come higher; but they, regarding what they had in commandment of the Prince, would not presume to do in any
thing contrary thereunto. He himself, only accompanied
with those of the King's house, was straight admitted to the
presence of the King his father, who, being at that time
grievously diseased, yet caused himself in his chair to be
borne into his privy chamber, where in the presence of
three or four persons in whom he had most confidence he
commanded the Prince to show what he had to say concern-
ing the cause of his coming.

The Prince, kneeling down before his father, said: "Most

---

63 nothing not at all   **64 reprove** disprove, confute   **65 terrets** rings by
which objects can be attached to a chain

redoubted[66] and sovereign lord and Father, I am at this time come to your presence as your liege man and as your natural son, in all things to be at your commandment. And where I understand you have in suspicion my demeanor against Your Grace, you know very well that if I knew any man within this realm of whom you should stand in fear, my duty were to punish that person, thereby to remove that grief from your heart. Then how much more ought I to suffer death, to ease Your Grace of that grief which you have of me, being your natural son and liege man, and to that end I have this day made myself ready by confession and receiving of the Sacrament. And therefore I beseech you, most redoubted lord and dear Father, for the honor of God, to ease your heart of all such suspicion as you have of me and to dispatch me here before your knees with this same dagger"—and withal he delivered unto the King his dagger, in all humble reverence, adding further that his life was not so dear to him that he wished to live one day with his displeasure—"and therefore in thus ridding me out of life and yourself from all suspicion, here in presence of these lords and before God at the day of the General Judgment, I faithfully protest clearly to forgive you."[67]

The King, moved herewith, cast from him the dagger and, embracing the Prince, kissed him and with shedding tears confessed that indeed he had him partly in suspicion, though now, as he perceived, not with just cause, and therefore from thenceforth no misreport should cause him to have him in mistrust, and this he promised of his honor. So by his great wisdom was the wrongful suspicion which his father had conceived against him removed and he restored to his favor. And further, where he could not but grievously complain of them that had slandered him so greatly, to the defacing not only of his honor but also putting him in danger of his life, he humbly besought the King that they might answer their unjust accusation, and in case they were found to have forged such matters upon a malicious purpose that then they might suffer some punishment for their faults, though not to the full of that they had deserved. The King, seeming to grant his reasonable desire, yet told him

66 redoubted reverenced, feared **67 forgive you** i.e., forgive you for killing me, if you choose to do so

that he must tarry[68] a parliament, that such offenders might
be punished by judgment of their peers; and so for that time
he was dismissed with great love and signs of fatherly affection.

Thus, were the father and the son reconciled, betwixt
whom the said pickthanks[69] had sown division, insomuch
that the son, upon a vehement conceit of unkindness
sprung in the father, was in the way to be worn out of favor.
Which was the more likely to come to pass by their informations that privily charged him with riot and other uncivil
demeanor unseemly for a prince. Indeed, he was youthfully
given, grown to audacity,[70] and had chosen him companions
agreeable to his age, with whom he spent the time in such
recreations, exercises, and delights as he fancied. But yet it
should seem by the report of some writers that his behavior
was not offensive or at least tending to the damage of anybody, sith he had a care to avoid doing of wrong and to
tether his affections within the tract[71] of virtue, whereby he
opened unto himself a ready passage of good liking among
the prudent sort and was beloved of such as could discern
his disposition, which was in no degree so excessive as that
he deserved in such vehement manner to be suspected. In
whose dispraise I find little but, to his praise very much.

The second edition of Raphael Holinshed's *Chronicles* was published in
1587. This selection is based on that edition, Volume 3, folios 518–539. Some
proper names have been modernized or regularized, including Glendower
(Glendouer), Almaine (Almane or Almanie), Cologne (Colin), Bavaria (Bauier),
Archibald (Archembald), Mordake (Mordacke), Murray (Murrey), Shirley
(Shorlie), Gawsey (Gausell), and Wensley (Wendesleie).

---

68 tarry await   **69 pickthanks** sycophants, talebearers   **70 audacity**
boldness, confidence   **71 tract** path, territory

The First Four Books of the Civil Wars Between the Two Houses of Lancaster and York (1595)
By Samuel Daniel

BOOK 3

[Bolingbroke, having become Henry IV, encounters military difficulties, especially with the Scots and Welsh.]

86

And yet new Hydras, lo, new heads appear
T'afflict that peace reputed then so sure,
And gave him much to do and much to fear,
And long and dangerous tumults did procure;
And those even of his chiefest followers were
Of whom he might presume him most secure,
Who, whether not so graced or so preferred
As they expected, these new factions stirred.

87

The Percys were the men, men of great might,
Strong in alliance and in courage strong,
That thus conspire under pretense to right
The crookèd courses they had suffered long;
Whether their conscience urged them or despite,
Or that they saw the part they took was wrong,
Or that ambition hereto did them call,
Or others envied grace, or rather all.

88

What cause soever were, strong was their plot,
Their parties great, means good, th' occasion fit;

86 · 1 Hydras (The Hydra was a mythical monster with many heads that grew again as soon as they were cut off.)   **7 whether** i.e., whether it was because they were

87 · 6 the part they took i.e., that their role in supporting Bolingbroke against Richard II, the legitimate king

Their practice close, their faith suspected not,
Their states far off and they of wary wit;
Who with large promises draw in the Scot
To aid their cause. He likes and yields to it,
Not for the love of them or for their good,
But glad hereby of means to shed our blood.

89

Then join they with the Welsh, who, fitly trained
And all in arms under a mighty head,
Great Glendower, who long warred and much attained,
Sharp conflicts made and many vanquishèd;
With whom was Edmund, Earl of March, retained,
Being first his prisoner, now confederèd,
A man the King much feared, and well he might
Lest he should look whether his crown stood right.

90

For Richard, for the quiet of the state,
Before he took those Irish wars in hand,
About succession doth deliberate,
And finding how the certain right did stand,
With full consent this man did ordinate
The heir apparent to the Crown and land.
Then judge if this the King might nearly touch,
Although his might were small, his right being much.

91

With these the Percys them confederate,
And as three heads they league in one intent,
And, instituting a triumvirate,

88 · 3 **Their practice close** their plotting secret   4 **Their states far off**
i.e., their estates far to the north in Northumberland   8 **our** i.e., English

89 · 6 **confederèd** allied, in league

90 · 5 **this man** i.e., Edmund, Earl of March. (But Daniel, like Holinshed,
and Shakespeare after them, conflates the fifth Earl of March, claimant
to the throne, with his uncle, Sir Edmund Mortimer, who was captured
by Glendower and married his daughter.)   **ordinate** name   7 **touch**
concern

91 · 1 **them confederate** ally themselves

Do part the land in triple government,
Dividing thus among themselves the state:
The Percys should rule all the North from Trent,
And Glendower Wales; the Earl of March should be
Lord of the South from Trent; and thus they 'gree.

92

Then those two helps which still such actors find—
Pretense of common good, the King's disgrace—
Doth fit their course and draw the vulgar mind
To further them and aid them in this case.
The King they accused for cruel and unkind,
That did the state, and Crown, and all deface—
A perjured man that held all faith in scorn,
Whose trusted oaths had others made forsworn.

93

Besides, the odious detestable act
Of that late murdered king they aggravate,
Making it his that so had willed the fact
That he the doers did remunerate,
And then such taxes daily doth exact
That were against the orders of the state;
And with all these, or worse, they him assailed
Who late of others with the like prevailed.

94

Thus doth contentious proud mortality
Afflict each other and itself torment.
And thus O thou, mind-torturing misery,
Restless Ambition, born in discontent,
Turn'st and retossest with iniquity
The unconstant courses frailty did invent,

92 • 1 still always   **3 vulgar** popular   **5 for** of being

93 • 3 his i.e., Bolingbroke's   **8 Who . . . prevailed** i.e., who himself only
recently succeeded in urging, along with others, similar complaints
against Richard II

94 • 1 mortality humankind

And foul'st fair order and defil'st the earth,
Fost'ring up War, father of blood and dearth.

95

Great seemed the cause, and greatly, too, did add
The peoples' love thereto, these crimes rehearsed,
That many gathered to the troops they had,
And many more do flock from coasts dispersed.
But when the King had heard these news so bad,
Th' unlooked-for dangerous toil more nearly pierced;
For, bent towards Wales t'appease those tumults there,
He's forced divert his course, and them forbear.

96

Not to give time unto th' increasing rage
And gathering fury, forth he hastes with speed,
Lest more delay, or giving longer age
To th' evil grown, it might the cure exceed.
All his best men at arms and leaders sage
All he prepared he could, and all did need;
For to a mighty work thou goest, O King,
To such a field that power to power shall bring.

97

There shall young Hotspur with a fury led
Meet with thy forward son as fierce as he;
There warlike Worcester, long experiencèd
In foreign arms, shall come t' encounter thee;
There Douglas to thy Stafford shall make head;

94 • 7 And foul'st and you befoul

95 • 4 from coasts dispersed i.e., from far and near   **8 them forbear** i.e., forbear fighting the Welsh

96 • 3–4 Lest . . . exceed i.e., lest further delay, giving rebellion time to ripen still more, might allow the disease to grow beyond the ability of means to cure it   **8 field** battlefield.   **power to power** army against army

97 • 2 forward ardent, eager   **4 In foreign arms** in fighting abroad
5 make head advance

There Vernon for thy valiant Blunt shall be.
There shalt thou find a doubtful bloody day,
Though sickness keep Northumberland away,

98

Who yet reserved, though after quit for this,
Another tempest on thy head to raise,
As if still-wrong revenging Nemesis
Did mean t' afflict all thy continual days.
And yet this field he happily might miss
For thy great good, and therefore well he stays.
What might his force have done, being joined thereto,
When that already gave so much to do?

99

The swift approach and unexpected speed
The King had made upon this new-raised force
In th' unconfirmèd troops much fear did breed,
Untimely hindering their intended course;
The joining with the Welsh they had decreed
Was hereby stopped, which made their part the worse;
Northumberland, with forces from the North
Expected to be there, was not set forth.

100

And yet undaunted Hotspur, seeing the King
So near approached, leaving the work in hand,
With forward speed his forces marshaling,
Sets forth his farther coming to withstand
And, with a cheerful voice encouraging
By his great spirit his well-emboldened band,
Brings a strong host of firm-resolvèd might
And placed his troops before the King in sight.

98·1 after quit subsequently requited **5 field** battlefield. **happily**
haply, perchance **6 For thy great good** i.e., a thing of great good fortune to you **8 When . . . do** i.e., when the rebel force, even without
Northumberland, gave so much trouble to Henry

99·3 unconfirmèd not knowing the rumor to be true for certain

101

"This day," saith he, "O faithful valiant friends,
Whatever it doth give, shall glory give.
This day with honor frees our state or ends
Our misery with fame, that still shall live.
And do but think how well this day he spends
That spends his blood his country to relieve!
Our holy cause, our freedom, and our right
Sufficient are to move good minds to fight.

102

"Besides, th' assurèd hope of victory
That we may even promise on our side
Against this weak constrainèd company
Whom force and fear, not will and love, doth guide,
Against a prince whose foul impiety
The heavens do hate, the earth cannot abide,
Our number being no less, our courage more,
What need we doubt if we but work therefor?"

103

This said, and thus resolved, even bent to charge
Upon the King, who well their order viewed
And careful noted all the form at large
Of their proceeding and their multitude;
And, deeming better if he could discharge
The day with safety and some peace conclude,
Great proffers sends of pardon and of grace
If they would yield and quietness embrace.

104

But this refused, the King, with wrath incensed,
Rage against fury doth with speed prepare.
And "O," saith he, "though I could have dispensed
With this day's blood, which I have sought to spare

---

101 · 5 he i.e., that person

102 · 3 constrainèd i.e., forced to fight on Henry's side, not willingly

103 · 1 even bent fully ready   **3 careful** carefully

That greater glory might have recompensed
The forward worth of these that so much dare,
That we might honor had by th' overthrown,
That th' wounds we make might not have been our own,

105

"Yet since that other men's iniquity
Calls on the sword of wrath against my will,
And that themselves exact this cruelty,
And I constrainèd am this blood to spill,
Then on, my masters! On courageously,
True-hearted subjects, against traitors ill,
And spare them not who seek to spoil us all,
Whose foul confusèd end soon see you shall!"

106

Straight moves with equal motion equal rage
The like incensèd armies unto blood,
One to defend, another side to wage
Foul civil war. Both vows their quarrel good.
Ah, too much heat to blood doth now enrage
Both who the deed provokes and who withstood,
That valor here is vice, here manhood sin.
The forward'st hands doth, O, least honor win.

107

But now begin these fury-moving sounds,
The notes of wrath that music brought from hell—
The rattling drums which trumpets' voice confounds,
The cries, th' encouragements, the shouting shrill—
That all about the beaten air rebounds,
Thund'ring confusèd, murmurs horrible,

104 • 7 had have had 8 our own i.e., English

105 • 1 since that since

106 • 1–2 Straight . . . blood immediately, with equal motion, an equal
rage moves these two armies, alike incensed, to bloodshed 6 Both . . .
provokes both those who provoke the deed 7–8 That . . . win i.e., in
civil war, valor and bravery prove dishonorable

To rob all sense except the sense to fight.
Well hands may work; the mind hath lost his sight.

108

O War! Begot in pride and luxury,
The child of wrath and of dissension,
Horrible good, mischief necessary,
The foul reformer of confusion,
Unjust-just scourge of our iniquity,
Cruel recurrer of corruption!
O that these sin-sick states in need should stand
To be let blood with such a boisterous hand!

109

And O, how well thou hadst been spared this day
Had not wrong-counseled Percy been perverse,
Whose young undangered hand now rash makes way
Upon the sharpest fronts of the most fierce;
Where now an equal fury thrusts to stay
And rebeat back that force and his disperse,
Then these assail, then those chase back again,
Till stayed with new-made hills of bodies slain.

110

There, lo! That new-appearing glorious star,
Wonder of arms, the terror of the field,
Young Henry, laboring where the stoutest are,
And even the stoutest forces back to yield;
There is that hand, boldened to blood and war,
That must the sword in woundrous actions wield.
But better hadst thou learned with others' blood,
A less expense to us, to thee more good.

107 · 8 his its

108 · 6 recurrer curer

109 · 1 thou i.e., War. **spared** avoided, done without **3 young undangered hand** i.e., young arm not yet tested in battle **4 fronts** points **5 stay** halt **6 rebeat back** beat back. **his disperse** disperse his (Percy's) troops

110 · 3 stoutest bravest **6 woundrous** wondrous (punning on *wound*)

111

Hadst thou not there lent present speedy aid
To thy endangered father, nearly tired,
Whom fierce encountering Douglas overlaid,
That day had there his troublous life expired.
Heroical courageous Blunt, arrayed
In habit like as was the King attired,
And deemed for him, excused that fate with his,
For he had what his lord did hardly miss.

112

For thought a king he would not now disgrace
The person then supposed, but princelike shows
Glorious effects of worth that fit his place,
And fighting dies, and dying overthrows.
Another of that forward name and race
In that hot work his valiant life bestows,
Who bare the standard of the King that day,
Whose colors overthrown did much dismay.

113

And dear it cost, and O, much blood is shed
To purchase thee this losing victory,
O travailed King. Yet hast thou conquerèd
A doubtful day, a mighty enemy.
But O, what wounds, what famous worth lies dead
That makes the winner look with sorrowing eye!
Magnanimous Stafford lost, that much had wrought,
And valiant Shirley, who great glory got.

---

111 · 1 present immediate   **7 excused . . . his** i.e., deflected King Henry's destined death onto his own   **8 For . . . miss** i.e., for he received what the King scarcely avoided, a death thrust

112 · 1–3 For . . . place i.e., buoyed up with the thought that he would not disgrace the royal person whom he impersonated, but instead in princelike fashion do glorious warlike deeds fitting a royal role
5–6 Another . . . bestows i.e., another Blunt also gives up his life in the heat of battle   **8 Whose . . . dismay** on which occasion the throwing down of the King's standard caused widespread dismay

113 · 3 travailed hard-pressed

114

Such wrack of others' blood thou didst behold,
O furious Hotspur, ere thou lost thine own!
Which now, once lost, that heat in thine waxed cold,
And soon became thy army overthrown;
And O, that this great spirit, this courage bold,
Had in some good cause been rightly shown!
So had not we thus violently then
Have termed that "rage" which "valor" should have
  been.

This selection is based on Samuel Daniel's *The First Four Books of the Civil Wars Between the Two Houses of Lancaster and York*, London, 1595.

The Famous Victories of Henry the Fifth, Containing the Honorable Battle of Agincourt

[Scene 1] *Enter the young Prince, Ned, and Tom [with stolen money].*

PRINCE Come away, Ned and Tom.

BOTH Here, my lord.

PRINCE Come away, my lads. Tell me, sirs, how much gold have you got?

NED Faith, my lord, I have got five hundred pound.

PRINCE But tell me, Tom, how much hast thou got?

TOM Faith, my lord, some four hundred pound.

PRINCE Four hundred pounds! Bravely spoken, lads. But tell me, sirs, think you not that it was a villainous part of me to rob my father's receivers?[1]

NED Why, no, my lord. It was but a trick of youth.

---

114 · 1 wrack devastation

Scene 1. Location: The highway south of London, about a mile from the city.
1 receivers treasury officials who receive or collect taxes

PRINCE Faith, Ned, thou sayest true. But tell me, sirs, whereabouts are we?

TOM My lord, we are now about a mile off London.

PRINCE But, sirs, I marvel that Sir John Oldcastle comes not away. Zounds,[2] see where he comes.

Enter Jockey[3] [*i.e., Sir John Oldcastle, with money*].

How now, Jockey, what news with thee?

SIR JOHN OLDCASTLE Faith, my lord, such news as passeth.[4] For the town of Deptford is risen with hue and cry after your man, which parted from us the last night and has set upon and hath robbed a poor carrier.[5]

PRINCE Zounds, the villain that was wont to spy out our booties?[6]

SIR JOHN OLDCASTLE Ay, my lord, even the very same.

PRINCE Now base-minded rascal, to rob a poor carrier! Well, it skills not.[7] I'll save the base villain's life. Ay, I may. But tell me, Jockey, whereabout be the receivers?

SIR JOHN OLDCASTLE Faith, my lord, they are hard by. But the best is we are ahorseback and they be afoot, so we may escape them.

PRINCE Well, if* the villains come, let me alone with them.[8] But tell me, Jockey, how much gots thou from the knaves? For I am sure I got something, for one of the villains so belammed[9] me about the shoulders as I shall feel it this month.

SIR JOHN OLDCASTLE Faith, my lord, I have got a hundred pound.

PRINCE A hundred pound! Now bravely spoken, Jockey. But come, sirs, lay all your money before me. [*They lay out the stolen money.*] Now, by heaven, here is a brave show! But, as I am true gentleman, I will have the half of this spent tonight. But, sirs, take up your bags. Here comes the receivers. [*They gather up the money.*] Let me alone.

Enters two Receivers.

FIRST RECEIVER [*To his companion*] Alas, good fellow, what

---

2 Zounds by his (God's) wounds **3 Jockey** Jack **4 passeth** surpasses
5 carrier one who hauls produce, a teamster **6 spy out our booties** act
as spy on our intended victims, our prizes **7 it skills not** it makes no
difference **8 let . . . them** let me handle them **9 belammed** beat

shall we do? I dare never go home to the court, for I shall be hanged. But look, here is the young Prince. What shall we do?

PRINCE   How now, you villains, what are you?

FIRST RECEIVER [*To his companion*]   Speak you to him.

SECOND RECEIVER   No, I pray, speak you to him.

PRINCE   Why, how now, you rascals, why speak you not?

FIRST RECEIVER   Forsooth, we be—pray, speak you to him.

PRINCE   Zounds, villains, speak, or I'll cut off your heads!

SECOND RECEIVER   Forsooth, he can tell the tale better than I.

FIRST RECEIVER   Forsooth, we be your father's receivers.

PRINCE   Are you my father's receivers? Then I hope ye have brought me some money.

FIRST RECEIVER   Money? Alas, sir, we be robbed!

PRINCE   Robbed! How many were there of them?

FIRST RECEIVER   Marry, sir, there were four of them. And one of them had Sir John Oldcastle's bay hobby[10] and your black nag.

PRINCE   Gog's wounds![11] How like you this, Jockey? Blood,[12] you villains, my father robbed of his money abroad, and we robbed in our stables! But tell me, how many were of them?

FIRST RECEIVER   If it please you, there were four of them. And there was one about the bigness of you, but I am sure I so belammed him about the shoulders that he will feel it this month.

PRINCE   Gog's wounds! You lammed them fairly, so that they have carried away your money. [*To his companions.*] But come, sirs, what shall we do with the villains?

BOTH RECEIVERS [*Kneeling*]   I beseech Your Grace, be good to us.

NED   I pray you, my lord, forgive them this once.

PRINCE*   Well, stand up and get you gone. And look that you speak not a word of it, for, if there be, zounds! I'll hang you and all your kin.   *Exit* [*Receivers*].*

Now, sirs, how like you this? Was not this bravely done? For now the villains dare not speak a word of it, I have so feared them with words. Now, whither shall we go?

ALL   Why, my lord, you know our old host's at Faversham.

PRINCE   Our host's at Faversham? Blood, what shall we do

---

10 hobby pony   **11 Gog's wounds** by God's wounds   **12 Blood** by God's blood there? We have a thousand pound about us, and we shall go to a petty alehouse? No, no. You know the old tavern in Eastcheap. There is good wine. Besides, there is a pretty wench that can talk well, for I delight as much in their tongues as any part[13] about them.

ALL   We are ready to wait upon[14] Your Grace.

PRINCE   Gog's wounds, "Wait"? We will go altogether; we are all fellows. I tell you, sirs, an[15] the King my father were dead, we would be all kings. Therefore, come away.

NED   Gog's wounds, bravely spoken, Harry!   [*Exeunt.*]

[Scene 2]   *Enter John Cobbler, Robin Pewterer, Lawrence Costermonger.*

JOHN   All is well here. All is well, masters.

LAWRENCE*   How say you, neighbor John Cobbler? I think it best that my neighbor, Robin Pewterer, went to Pudding Lane End, and we will watch here at Billingsgate Ward.[1] How say you, neighbor Robin? How like you this?

ROBIN   Marry, well, neighbors. I care not much if I go to Pudding Lane's End. But, neighbors, an you hear any ado about me, make haste; and if I hear any ado about you, I will come to you.   *Exit Robin.*

LAWRENCE   Neighbor, what news hear you of the young Prince?

JOHN   Marry, neighbor, I hear say he is a toward[2] young prince; for, if he meet any by the highway, he will not let[3] to talk with[4] him. I dare not call him thief, but sure he is one of these taking fellows.[5]

LAWRENCE   Indeed, neighbor, I hear say he is as lively a young prince as ever was.

JOHN   Ay, and I hear say if he use it long, his father will cut him off from the Crown. But, neighbor, say nothing of that!

---

13 part (with bawdy suggestion)   **14 wait upon** attend   **15 an** if

Scene 2. Location: London, near Eastcheap, at night.
1 Pudding Lane End, Billingsgate Ward (Places between Eastcheap and the Thames River. The men here are part of the night watch.)   **2 toward** (1) promising (2) quick to learn tricks   **3 let** hesitate, pass up the opportunity   **4 talk with** (1) converse with (2) rob   **5 taking fellows** (1) engaging chaps (2) robbers

LAWRENCE   No, no, neighbor, I warrant you.

JOHN   Neighbor, methinks you begin to sleep. If you will, we will sit down, for I think it is about midnight.

LAWRENCE   Marry, content, neighbor. Let us sleep.

Enter Derick, roving.[6]

DERICK   Who? Who there, who there?[7]   *Exit Derick.*

Enter Robin.

ROBIN   O neighbors, what mean you to sleep, and such ado in the streets?

BOTH   How now, neighbor, what's the matter?

Enter Derick again.

DERICK   Who there? Who there? Who there?

JOHN   Why, what ailst thou? Here is no horses.[8]

DERICK   O, alas, man, I am robbed! Who there? Who there?

ROBIN   Hold him, neighbor Cobbler. Why, I see thou art a plain clown.[9]

DERICK   Am I a clown? Zounds, masters, do clowns go in silk apparel? I am sure all we gentlemen-clowns in Kent scant go so well. Zounds, you know clowns very well. Hear you, are you Master Constable? An[10] you be, speak, for I will not take it at his hands.[11]

JOHN   Faith, I am not Master Constable, but I am one of his bad[12] officers, for he is not here.

DERICK   Is not Master Constable here? Well, it is no matter. I'll have the law at his hands.[13]

JOHN   Nay, I pray you, do not take the law of us.[14]

DERICK   Well, you are one of his beastly[15] officers.

JOHN   I am one of his bad officers.

DERICK   Why, then, I charge thee, look to him![16]

---

6 roving wandering about   **7 who there** i.e., is anybody there? (Derick, a poor carrier who has been robbed, is looking for help.)   **8 Here is no horses** (John Cobbler evidently thinks Derick is calling out for someone from whom he can hire horses.)   **9 clown** rustic countryman, bumpkin   **10 An** if   **11 take it at his hands** take it from him, believe his word   **12 bad** (1) poor, unworthy, humble (2) *bade*, bidden to serve   **13 at his hands** from him (the Constable) directly   **14 take the law of** invoke the law on (playing on the meaning in the previous speech)   **15 beastly** (playing on the normal meaning of *bad*)   **16 look to him** i.e., look to the thief (?)

JOHN   Nay, but hear ye, sir. You seem to be an honest fellow, and we are poor men; and now 'tis night, and we would be loath to have anything ado.[17] Therefore, I pray thee, put it up.[18]

DERICK   First, thou sayest true. I am an honest fellow, and a proper,[19] handsome fellow, too. And you seem to be poor men; therefore I care not greatly. Nay, I am quickly pacified. But, an you chance to spy the thief, I pray you lay hold on him.

ROBIN   Yes, that we will, I warrant you.

DERICK   'Tis a wonderful thing to see how glad the knave is, now I have forgiven him.

JOHN   Neighbors, do ye look about you.[20] How now, who's there?

Enter the Thief.

THIEF   Here is a good fellow. I pray you, which is the way to the old tavern in Eastcheap?

DERICK   Whoop halloo! Now, Gad's Hill,[21] knowest thou me?

THIEF   I know thee for an ass.

DERICK   And I know thee for a taking fellow upon Gad's Hill in Kent. A bots[22] light upon ye.

THIEF   The whoreson villain would be knocked.[23]

DERICK   Masters, villain! An ye be men, stand to him and take his weapon from him. Let him not pass you!

JOHN   My friend, what make you abroad[24] now? It is too late to walk now.

THIEF   It is not too late for true men to walk.

LAWRENCE   We know thee not to be a true man.

                                        [*They seize the Thief.*]

THIEF   Why, what do you mean to do with me? Zounds! I am one of the King's liege people.[25]

DERICK   Hear you, sir, are you one of the King's liege people?

THIEF   Ay, marry am I, sir. What say you to it?

---

17 ado amiss   **18 put it up** i.e., pocket up your complaint   **19 proper** good-looking   **20 look about you** look sharp   **21 Gad's Hill** (The name of a place in Kent notorious for highway robberies, here applied to the Thief, as also in Shakespeare's play.)   **22 bots** (Literally, a disease in horses caused by parasites; here, an expression of execration.)   **23 The whoreson . . . knocked** i.e., the rascally knave (Derick) is asking for a blow   **24 make you abroad** are you doing out and around   **25 liege people** loyal subjects

DERICK   Marry, sir, I say you are one of the King's filching
people.

JOHN   Come, come. Let's have him away.

THIEF   Why, what have I done?

ROBIN   Thou hast robbed a poor fellow and taken away his
goods from him.

THIEF   I never saw him before.

DERICK   Masters, who comes here?

Enter the Vintner's Boy.

BOY   How now, goodman Cobbler?

JOHN   How now, Robin, what makes thou abroad at this time
of night?

BOY   Marry, I have been at the Counter.[26] I can tell such news
as never you have heard the like.

JOHN   What is that, Robin? What is the matter?

BOY   Why, this night, about two hours ago, there came the
young Prince and three or four more of his companions, and
called for wine good store,[27] and then they sent for a noise[28]
of musicians and were very merry for the space of an hour.
Then, whether their music liked them not,[29] or whether they
had drunk too much wine or no, I cannot tell, but our pots
flew against the walls. And then they drew their swords and
went into the street and fought, and some took one part and
some took another, but for the space of half an hour there
was such a bloody fray as passeth![30] And none could part
them until such time as the Mayor and Sheriff were sent for.
And then at the last with much ado they took them, and so
the young Prince was carried to the Counter. And then about
one hour after there came a messenger from the court in all
haste from the King for my Lord Mayor and the Sheriff, but
for what cause I know not.

JOHN   Here is news, indeed, Robert!

LAWRENCE   Marry, neighbor, this news is strange indeed. I
think it best, neighbor, to rid our hands of this fellow first.

THIEF   What mean you to do with me?

JOHN   We mean to carry you to the prison, and there to
remain[31] till the sessions day.

---

26 the Counter a London prison   **27 good store** in abundant quantity
28 noise consort, band   **29 liked them not** displeased them   **30 passeth**
surpasses belief   **31 and there to remain** and you to remain there

THIEF   Then, I pray you, let me go to the prison where my master[32] is.

JOHN   Nay, thou must go to the country prison,[33] to Newgate. Therefore, come away.

THIEF   [*To Derick*]   I prithee, be good to me, honest fellow.

DERICK   Ay, marry, will I. I'll be very charitable to thee, for I will never leave thee till I see thee on the gallows.

                                                                    [*Exeunt.*]

[The subsequent scenes, in which Prince Henry boxes the ear of the Lord Chief Justice, is imprisoned by him, and is at last reconciled with his dying father, are materials for *2 Henry IV* and are printed as sources for that play.]

———————————

This selection is based on the first edition of *The Famous Victories of Henry the Fifth, Containing the Honorable Battle of Agincourt; As It Was Played by the Queen's Majesty's Players. London: Printed by Thomas Creede, 1598.* [Designated in the textual notes below as Q.]

In the following, departures from the original text appear in boldface; original readings are in roman. (The speech prefixes have been silently regularized.)

p. 141 *if I [Q]   p. 142 s.p. *Prince [not in Q]   p. 142 s.d. *Exit [Receivers] Exit Purseuant [Q]   p. 143 s.p. *Lawrence Robin [Q]

———————————

32 my master i.e., Prince Henry   33 the country prison i.e., the prison not under the jurisdiction of the city of London as was the Counter. (The Thief has been apprehended in Kent.)

Further Reading

Auden, W. H. "The Prince's Dog." *The Dyer's Hand and Other Essays.* New York: Random House, 1948. Auden inventively examines Falstaff's character, motives, and function within the play, and concludes that "sober reflection in the study may tell us that Falstaff is not, after all, a very admirable person, but Falstaff on the stage gives us no time for sober reflection." Auden denies the damaging irresponsibility many critics have found in Falstaff, declaring him to be "a comic symbol for the supernatural order of charity."

Barber, C. L. "Rule and Misrule in *Henry IV.*" *Shakespeare's Festive Comedy.* Princeton, N.J.: Princeton Univ. Press, 1959. In his seminal study of the relation of social and artistic forms, Barber sees Falstaff as a Lord of Misrule burlesquing the sanctities of the historical world. Barber finds, however, that misrule does not threaten the social order, since "it depends utterly on what it mocks." Ultimately "misrule works . . . to consolidate rule," though Falstaff's saturnalian energy always threatens to turn from a "dependent holiday skepticism" to a "dangerously self-sufficient everyday skepticism."

Barish, Jonas A. "The Turning Away of Prince Hal." *Shakespeare Studies* 1 (1965): 9–17. Barish sees Falstaff's rejection as the moment that reveals to us whether we are "moralists or sentimentalists"; we also sense at this moment the antithetical pressures of history and comedy. In rejecting Falstaff, Hal is, in effect, rejecting himself: "to banish plump Jack is to banish what is free and vital and pleasurable in life."

Bradley, A. C. "The Rejection of Falstaff." *Oxford Lectures on Poetry,* 1909. Rpt. New York: St. Martin's Press, 1959. Bradley's influential essay explores the inevitability of Hal's rejection of Falstaff. He recognizes both Falstaff's dangerous attractiveness and Hal's Lancastrian "hardness" that qualifies him for political success but limits his personal appeal. If we enjoy the Falstaff scenes "as surely Shakespeare meant for them to be enjoyed," Bradley argues, we must feel in Falstaff's rejection "a good deal of pain and some resentment."

Brooks, Cleanth, and Robert B. Heilman. "Shakespeare, *Henry IV, Part I.*" *Understanding Drama.* New York: Holt, Rinehart, and Winston, 1945. For Brooks and Heilman, the play is a "study in the nature of kingship" in which Hal must choose a course of action from among the models offered him by his father, Falstaff, and Hotspur. Brooks and Heilman explore the careful balance of sympathies established by the play that lead an audience "to contemplate, with understanding and some irony, a world very much like the world we know."

Burckhardt, Sigurd. " 'Swoll'n with Some Other Grief': Shakespeare's Prince Hal Trilogy." *Shakespearean Meanings.* Princeton, N.J.: Princeton Univ. Press, 1968. Burckhardt argues that the structure of Shakespeare's plays "undercuts Tudor doctrine," exposing its contradictions and inadequacies. The apparently satisfying resolution of *1 Henry IV* dissolves as Falstaff rises from the battlefield, "reminding us that disorder is not slain so neatly and inexpensively as the calculated symmetries of dialectics would have us believe."

Calderwood, James L. "*1 Henry IV:* Art's Gilded Lie." *Metadrama in Shakespeare's Henriad: "Richard II" to "Henry V."* Berkeley and Los Angeles: Univ. of California Press, 1979. Calderwood ingeniously explores the metadramatic implications of Hal's lie supporting Falstaff's claim to have killed Hotspur. What is at stake, Calderwood argues, is "theatrical illusion itself." Hal, who historically must unify a country torn by dissension, must reunite a play threatening to split into competing dramatic modes. Falstaff, in his outrageous theatricality, threatens to withdraw from the play's mimesis of history, and Hal's lie is necessary to persuade him to remain within the historical action.

Campbell, Lily B. "The Unquiet Time of Henry IV." *Shakespeare's "Histories": Mirrors of Elizabethan Policy.* San Marino, Calif.: Huntington Library, 1947. Campbell considers the historical action of the play in the context of Elizabethan political theory and anxieties about succession. She argues that "the problem of rebellion" is central to the design of *Henry IV* and reflects the realities of sixteenth-century politics as much as the medieval history overtly represented.

Council, Norman. "*1 Henry IV:* The Mirror up to Nature." *When Honour's at the Stake: Ideas of Honour in Shakespeare's Plays.* London: George Allen and Unwin; New York: Barnes and Noble, 1973. Council argues that the theme of honor is central to the play, but denies that Hotspur and Falstaff represent moral extremes for Hal to mediate. Council's reading of both the play and sixteenth-century ethical treatises and courtesy books reveals Hotspur to be the "true and perfect image of honor," Falstaff the embodiment of "the nature and consequences of a reasoned rejection of the pervasive code of honor," and Hal one who neither simply accepts nor rejects the code but successfully "exploits it for his pragmatic purposes."

Dessen, Alan C. "Dual Protagonists in *1 Henry IV.*" *Shakespeare and the Late Moral Plays.* Lincoln, Nebr., and London: Univ. of Nebraska Press, 1986. Dessen finds in the dramaturgy of the late morality plays of the 1560s and 1570s a structural model for *1 Henry IV.* In the dual protagonists of plays such as *The Trial of Treasure* (1567), Shakespeare finds a prototype for his pairing of Hal and Hotspur, who enact "far more complex versions" of the morality action.

Greenblatt, Stephen. "Invisible Bullets: Renaissance Authority and Its Subversion." *Glyph* 8 (1981): 40–61. Rev. and rpt. in *Political Shakespeare: New Essays in Cultural Materialism,* ed. Jonathan Dollimore and Alan Sinfield. Ithaca and London: Cornell Univ. Press, 1985. Greenblatt considers the *Henry IV* plays in a provocative account of the operations of Renaissance power. He argues that the subversive challenge to the principles of authority in the play is never really dangerous; indeed, it is not merely contained but actually encouraged by the power structure, since its presence works paradoxically to ratify and reinforce the existing order.

Hunter, G. K. "*Henry IV* and the Elizabethan Two-Part Play." *Review of English Studies* n. s. 5 (1954): 236–248. Rpt. in *Dramatic Identities and Cultural Tradition: Stud-*

ies in Shakespeare and His Contemporaries. New York: Barnes and Noble, 1978. Entering into the debate about the relationship of the two parts of *Henry IV,* Hunter argues not that the two plays are continuous but that they have the unity, found also in plays by Christopher Marlowe, John Marston, and George Chapman, "of a dyptich, in which repetition of shape and design focuses attention on what is common to the two parts."

Kelly, Henry Ansgar. *Divine Providence in the England of Shakespeare's Histories,* pp. 214–222. Cambridge: Harvard Univ. Press, 1970. Examining the play's often noted "providentialism," Kelly finds that the "moral and providential judgments of the sources" are not normative but are distributed in the play according to the partisan uses that can be made of them. He denies there is any evidence that the play enacts "the providential punishment of Henry IV" for the deposition of Richard II. Henry "regards himself as the rightful king," and if the play suggests divine support for anyone, "that person is Henry IV."

Kernan, Alvin B. "The Henriad: Shakespeare's Major History Plays." In *Modern Shakespearean Criticism: Essays on Style, Dramaturgy, and the Major Plays,* ed. Alvin B. Kernan. New York: Harcourt, Brace and World, 1970. Kernan traces the movement of the second tetralogy from a sacred, providential conception of history to a secular, pragmatic view, "in which any identity is only a temporary role." Richard II, Henry IV, and Prince Hal mark stages in this transition, and the latter emerges as the modern prince who "never seems to lose sight of the fact he is preparing to be king of England."

Morgann, Maurice. "An Essay on the Dramatic Character of Sir John Falstaff" (1777). In *Eighteenth Century Essays on Shakespeare,* 2nd edition, ed. D. Nichol Smith. Oxford: Clarendon Press, 1963. In an essay that is the earliest sustained account of a Shakespearean character, Morgann sees the complexity of Falstaff's nature as it is presented in the play. He is not the "constitutional coward" that many have seen but a man "of much natural courage and resolution." Morgann, however, recognizes that if Falstaff is endowed with "great natural vigour and alacrity of mind," he also engages "in every debauchery." He has "a mind free of malice or any evil principle; but he never took the trouble of acquiring any good one."

Ornstein, Robert. *"Henry IV Part I."* *A Kingdom for a Stage: The Achievement of Shakespeare's History Plays.* Cambridge: Harvard Univ. Press, 1972. Examining the "illogic of human motive" that lies "behind the logic of events" in the play, Ornstein sensitively examines the roles "which personality and circumstance dictate" to its characters. At the center of the analysis is Hal, and Ornstein finds him "fascinating but not endearing," incapable of intimacy, shrewd, and pragmatic: "he studies other men so that he may learn to master them."

Porter, Joseph A. *"1 Henry IV."* *The Drama of Speech Acts: Shakespeare's Lancastrian Tetralogy.* Berkeley, Calif.: Univ. of California Press, 1979. Porter examines the various "ways of conceiving and using language" in the play: King Henry's "inexplicitness," Hotspur's "energetic noncommunication," Falstaff's "refusal to converse responsibly," and Prince Hal's efforts to master "the variety of languages" of the realm, a mastery necessary for his eventual rule.

Reese, M. M. *"Henry IV."* *The Cease of Majesty: A Study of Shakespeare's History Plays.* London: Edward Arnold, 1961; New York: St. Martin's Press, 1962. Reese argues that Shakespeare in the two parts of *Henry IV* dramatizes "the education of a prince" and "considers in personal and political terms the sacrifices and disciplines [Hal] will have to accept." Reese considers Falstaff, Hotspur, and Henry IV to be "three tempters" whose defective examples Hal must reject as his youthful impulses are "steeled into disciplined courage and dedicated to honourable ends."

Saccio, Peter. "Henry IV: The King Embattled." *Shakespeare's English Kings: History, Chronicle, and Drama.* New York: Oxford Univ. Press, 1977. Focusing especially on the political challenges to Henry's rule, the military encounters at Shrewsbury and Gaultree Forest, and the relations between Henry IV and his son, Saccio examines the historical background of the two parts of *Henry IV,* and traces Shakespeare's transformation of this history into drama.

Tillyard, E. M. W. "The Second Tetralogy." *Shakespeare's History Plays*, 1944. Rpt., New York: Barnes and Noble, 1964. In an enormously influential study of Shakespeare's histories, Tillyard argues that the two parts of *Henry IV* form a single sequence of ten acts in which Hal is tested, "Morality-fashion," to prove his worthiness to rule. *Part One* demonstrates Hal's education in military virtues, as he tries to mediate between "the excess and the defect of the military spirit" as they are embodied in Hotspur and Falstaff; *Part Two* displays his education in the "civil virtues," as he must choose between Falstaff and the Lord Chief Justice.

Memorable Lines

So shaken as we are, so wan with care . . .   (KING   1.1.1)

. . . thy quips and thy quiddities?   (FALSTAFF   1.2.43–44)

. . . so far as my coin would stretch, and where it would not I
have used my credit.   (PRINCE   1.2.53–54)

O, thou hast damnable iteration, and art indeed able to corrupt a saint.   (FALSTAFF   1.2.89–90)

Now am I, if a man should speak truly, little better than one
of the wicked.   (FALSTAFF   1.2.92–94)

'Tis my vocation, Hal. 'Tis no sin for a man to labor in his
vocation.   (FALSTAFF   1.2.102–103)

There's neither honesty, manhood, nor good fellowship in
thee.   (FALSTAFF   1.2.136–137)

If all the year were playing holidays,
To sport would be as tedious as to work.
     (PRINCE   1.2.198–199)

To put down Richard, that sweet lovely rose,
And plant this thorn, this canker, Bolingbroke?
     (HOTSPUR   1.3.175–176)

Have you any levers to lift me up again, being down?
     (FALSTAFF   2.2.33–34)

Go hang thyself in thine own heir-apparent garters!
     (FALSTAFF   2.2.42–43)

Young men must live.   (FALSTAFF   2.2.90)

                    Falstaff sweats to death
And lards the lean earth as he walks along.
     (PRINCE   2.2.107–108)

Out of this nettle, danger, we pluck this flower, safety.

(HOTSPUR   2.3.9–10)

This is no world
To play with mammets and to tilt with lips.

(HOTSPUR   2.3.90–91)

A plague of all cowards!   (FALSTAFF   2.4.116–117)

There is nothing but roguery to be found in villainous man.

(FALSTAFF   2.4.122–123)

Watch tonight, pray tomorrow.   (FALSTAFF   2.4.273–274)

What doth Gravity out of his bed at midnight?

(FALSTAFF   2.4.291)

You may buy land now as cheap as stinking mackerel.

(FALSTAFF   2.4.356–357)

Him keep with, the rest banish.   (FALSTAFF   2.4.425–426)

Why dost thou converse with that trunk of humors, that
bolting-hutch of beastliness . . . that reverend Vice, that gray
Iniquity, that father ruffian, that vanity in years?

(PRINCE   2.4.443–449)

If to be fat be to be hated, then Pharaoh's lean kine are to be
loved.   (FALSTAFF   2.4.467–468)

. . . but for sweet Jack Falstaff . . . banish not him thy Harry's
company—banish plump Jack, and banish all the world.

(FALSTAFF   2.4.470–475)

I am not in the roll of common men.   (GLENDOWER   3.1.41)

Tell truth and shame the devil.   (HOTSPUR   3.1.56)

I have more flesh than another man, and therefore more
frailty.   (FALSTAFF   3.3.167–169)

I saw young Harry, with his beaver on ... (VERNON 4.1.104)

What is honor? A word. What is in that word "honor"? What is that "honor"? Air. A trim reckoning!

(FALSTAFF 5.1.133–135)

Honor is a mere scutcheon. And so ends my catechism.

(FALSTAFF 5.1.139–140)

... the time of life is short!
To spend that shortness basely were too long.

(HOTSPUR 5.2.81–82)

Give me life, which if I can save, so; if not, honor comes unlooked for, and there's an end. (FALSTAFF 5.3.59–61)

The better part of valor is discretion.

(FALSTAFF 5.4.119–120)

Lord, Lord, how this world is given to lying!

(FALSTAFF 5.4.143–144)

Contributors

DAVID BEVINGTON, Phyllis Fay Horton Professor of Humanities at the University of Chicago, is editor of *The Complete Works of Shakespeare* (Scott, Foresman, 1980) and of *Medieval Drama* (Houghton Mifflin, 1975). His latest critical study is *Action Is Eloquence: Shakespeare's Language of Gesture* (Harvard University Press, 1984).

DAVID SCOTT KASTAN, Professor of English and Comparative Literature at Columbia University, is the author of *Shakespeare and the Shapes of Time* (University Press of New England, 1982).

JAMES HAMMERSMITH, Associate Professor of English at Auburn University, has published essays on various facets of Renaissance drama, including literary criticism, textual criticism, and printing history.

ROBERT KEAN TURNER, Professor of English at the University of Wisconsin–Milwaukee, is a general editor of the New Variorum Shakespeare (Modern Language Association of America) and a contributing editor to *The Dramatic Works in the Beaumont and Fletcher Canon* (Cambridge University Press, 1966–).

JAMES SHAPIRO, who coedited the bibliographies with David Scott Kastan, is Assistant Professor of English at Columbia University.

❦

JOSEPH PAPP, one of the most important forces in theater today, is the founder and producer of the New York Shakespeare Festival, America's largest and most prolific theatrical institution. Since 1954 Mr. Papp has produced or directed all but one of Shakespeare's plays—in Central Park, in schools, off and on Broadway, and at the Festival's permanent home, The Public Theater. He has also produced such award-winning plays and musical works as *Hair, A Chorus Line, Plenty,* and *The Mystery of Edwin Drood,* among many others.

THE BANTAM SHAKESPEARE COLLECTION

The Complete Works in 28 Volumes

Edited with Introductions by David Bevington

Forewords by Joseph Papp

Ask for these books at your local bookstore or use this page to order.

Please send me the books I have checked above. I am enclosing $_____ (add $2.50 to cover postage and handling). Send check or money order, no cash or C.O.D.'s, please.

Name _____

Address _____

City/State/Zip _____

Send order to: Bantam Books, Dept. SH 2, 2451 S. Wolf Rd., Des Plaines, IL 60018
Allow four to six weeks for delivery.

Prices and availability subject to change without notice.   SH 2 2/99